D0873987

21040

PAKISTAN

THE HEART OF ASIA

SPEECHES BY LIAQUAT ALI KHAN

PAKISTAN

THE HEART OF ASIA

Speeches in the United States and Canada
May and June 1950 - by the
Prime Minister of Pakistan

LIAQUAT ALI KHAN

WITH AN APPENDIX BY BEGUM LIAQUAT ALI KHAN

HARVARD UNIVERSITY PRESS
Cambridge, Massachusetts
1950

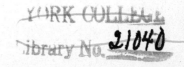
YORK COLLEGE
Library No. 21040

DS
385
.K5
A25

Copyright 1950

By the President and Fellows of Harvard College

Distributed in Great Britain by

Geoffrey Cumberlege

Oxford University Press

Printed in the United States of America

PUBLISHERS' FOREWORD

Pakistan, The Heart of Asia is a volume composed primarily of the speeches made by Liaquat Ali Khan, Prime Minister of Pakistan, during his brief trip to the United States and Canada in May and June 1950. With the addresses of the Prime Minister are printed also a very few of the introductory or commentative speeches made by distinguished citizens of the two countries to audiences the Prime Minister was addressing. Liaquat Ali Khan and the publishers hoped at first that all the public remarks made by Canadians and Americans about his visit could be included in the volume, but this hope has proved impracticable. In the first place, not all the texts have been available since some were given extemporaneously; secondly, it was soon realized that to print all that were available would change the book from a small and inexpensive volume to a larger and much more costly one—an alteration that would have interfered with the objective of presenting Liaquat Ali Khan's message of peace and goodwill to the maximum reading public. A consideration of this kind, it is believed, will be readily understood. To those kind and hospitable individuals whose generously given words are thus not used in this book, as well as to those whose statements are included, the Prime Minister and his publishers offer their most sincere thanks.

As is true of any series of speeches given in a brief period by one man, the same topics necessarily recurred from time to time in Liaquat Ali Khan's remarks. To avoid repetition and unnecessary

v

length the texts of these talks, particularly those given during the latter part of his visit, have been very considerably abridged, such abridgments being noted in the usual way.

The publishers take special pleasure in offering as an appendix to the volume the speech given at Town Hall, New York, by Begum Liaquat Ali Khan, wife of the Prime Minister. The remarkable change which has taken place in the life of the Muslim women of Asia in the last few years could not be more dramatically expressed than in the words of the Begum, the leader in the development.

The reader will note that the spelling and punctuation of the Prime Minister and the Begum, both of whom follow British usage, differ from the spelling and punctuation of the Americans quoted. No effort has been made to reduce these matters to a standard, British or American, as it was thought wisest to leave in every speaker's words as much of his own flavor as possible. The publishers hope that this lack of consistency will not be disconcerting to any reader.

TJW

CONTENTS

PREFACE

This book is a record of the speeches made by the Prime Minister Liaquat Ali Khan, together with the welcoming addresses of his American hosts when, accompanied by his distinguished and charming wife, Begum Liaquat Ali Khan, he visited the United States in May 1950. The visit expressed, and was meant to express publicly, what the two governments had long believed—that though Pakistan and America are far apart in space, though they are very different in their ways of life, each has great responsibilities for the peace and welfare of mankind which it cannot hope to meet fully without the advice and help of the other.

The visit did much more, however, than to express this belief. The Americans who met the Prime Minister and had a chance to learn the quality of the man and the breadth and freedom of his ideas were left with the feeling that the collaboration which was so obviously desirable was no mere pious hope, but one of the great positive elements of the modern world.

It is not easy to exaggerate how much depends upon whether this collaboration is realized. The relationship between the Western World and Asia, which began with the European imperial conquests some four centuries ago, is in its very last phase. As the old empires have dissolved, the problem of the succession has arisen. In most of Asia, in what we call the Far East particularly, the problem of the succession is not solved. But in southern Asia, in the enormous subcontinent, the problem has been solved by the emergence of two powerful, two pacific, two sovereign Asiatic states—India and Pakistan.

With these states on a basis of absolute equality and, in addition, with a sense of humility we, who have never been an empire, must with tireless patience seek to work out the new relationship between Asia and the Western World. This is an enormous, a momentous, a fascinating, and a rewarding work. The reader of this book will find in it a good introduction to this task—to this the most interesting creative undertaking of the Twentieth Century.

July 10, 1950

Walter Lippmann

WELCOME IN WASHINGTON

In response to President Harry S. Truman's cordial invitation, Prime Minister Liaquat Ali Khan of Pakistan and the Begum visited the United States in May 1950. They arrived by plane at the Washington National Airport on 3 May. President Truman's speech of welcome follows:

Mr. Prime Minister, Begum Sahiba: With a deep sense of the historical import of this occasion, and with the greatest personal pleasure, I am happy to welcome you both to the United States. Mrs. Truman and I, and Americans throughout our country, have been looking forward to your arrival. We are glad you have found it possible to do us the honor of visiting us, and are thankful that you have been granted a safe journey.

The many Americans who have had the privilege of visiting Pakistan are unanimous in their praise of your heart-warming hospitality. I hope that while you are in the United States you will feel as much at home as Americans do when they visit your great country. It is likewise my sincere hope that in the course of your stay you will find that Americans and Pakistanis have much in common.

Knowing that the number of invitations from Americans wishing to extend hospitality has far exceeded the number which your sojourn in the United States will permit you to accept, I wish at this time to extend a warm and heartfelt welcome on behalf of all the American people.

The reply of Prime Minister Liaquat Ali Khan to Mr. Truman's welcoming speech, 3 May 1950.

Mr. President: My wife and I are deeply grateful to you and Mrs. Truman for your warm and generous welcome. In extending your

2

traditional hospitality to us, you and the people of the United States of America have done great honour to us and to our country.

I bring you and the great American nation the most friendly greetings of eighty million men and women of Pakistan. Although we come from a distant country in the heart of Asia, and this is my first visit to your land, the American people are not strangers to us. We have known them as educators and as men and women engaged on missions of peace. We have known them as soldiers who fought for freedom in our plains, our hills and our jungles. And again since the birth of Pakistan we have known them as messengers of your goodwill.

I know that my wife and I will be very happy here and that we shall carry back to our people memories not only of the greatness of your purposes but also of the greatness of your hearts.

May God who has brought us safely across to your shores bless our hosts and their homes.

On the morning of 4 May 1950, the Prime Minister spoke to the Senate of the United States. He was introduced by Vice-President Alben S. Barkley, President of the Senate, who said:

Members of the Senate, we are honored today by a visit from the Prime Minister of Pakistan. The whole world knows the process by which in recent years India and Pakistan, which were originally united as India, have acquired their independence.

We are glad to welcome the Prime Minister of Pakistan, which originally was a part of India, and which, through negotiation and friendly cooperation, has become a free and independent nation, as free and independent as India itself is at this time.

We are glad to welcome to the Senate any representative of freedom-loving, self-governing, and independent people; and particularly are we happy to welcome the Prime Minister of Pakistan, His Excellency Liaquat Ali Khan, whom I have the pleasure now to present to the Senate, and who will address us.

3

PAKISTAN: THE AIMS OF A NEW NATION

In welcoming me within these walls and giving me an opportunity of addressing this august assembly, you have bestowed upon me high prerogative and honour for which I am deeply grateful to you.

This is my first visit to your great land, but I have long been an admirer of the vigour of your enterprise, your indefatigable spirit of enquiry, your optimism, your high respect for individual effort, your belief in equal opportunities for all, your reverence for the sanctity of the home, the frankness of your speech and manner and the liveliness of your language. Above all, I have admired your zealous and un-compromising regard for the supremacy of the people's will, your firm belief that civil liberty gives man the greatest scope for his faculties and your faith that "morality is the best security of law and the surest pledge of freedom." In seeing America, I hope to see more than America. I hope to see the men and women whose enterprise and vitality have made your country great and the faith that sustains them in their efforts.

I thank you for your welcome and value it the more, because the people whom I have the honour and privilege to represent, although the inheritors of ancient faiths and cultures, are, as a nation among sovereign nations, young and on the threshold of new experiences, both exciting and grave.

In the geography of the world, Pakistan's name is not yet three years old. What led to the emergence of this new State on the map of Asia is perhaps not universally known. Nor do I expect it yet to be common knowledge what urges stir and inspire us in the task that we know lies ahead of us.

Pakistan was founded by the indomitable will of a hundred mil-

4

THE PRIME MINISTER OF PAKISTAN

THE BEGUM

lion Muslims who felt that they were a nation too numerous and too distinct to be relegated forever to the unalterable position of a political minority, specially when, in the vast subcontinent which was their homeland, there was enough room for two great nations— the Hindus and the Muslims—to enjoy peace and full sovereignty in their respective dominions. They believed that thus alone would the vast multitude of the followers of Islam be uninhibited in the development of their culture and free to follow their own way of life. Pakistan was founded so that millions of Muslims should be enabled to live according to their opinions and to worship God in freedom. That self-same freedom which they sought for themselves they conceded to others, with the determination to live as peaceful neighbours when to live as more than neighbours seemed to be more than hazardous. Like some of the earlier founders of your great country, these Muslims, though not Pilgrims, nevertheless embarked upon an undertaking, which, in aim and achievement, represented the triumph of an idea. That idea was the idea of liberty which has had its ardent followers in all climates and all countries. When our time came, its call summoned us too, and we could not hold back. The partition of our subcontinent into two independent sovereign States did not, nor was it expected to, eliminate or efface minorities. But it brought magnitudes within focusable limits and saved the political architecture of the new Asia from a strain which might well have proved excessive and dangerous.

But this, we realize, is only the beginning of a new life. The achievement of freedom is not an instantaneous event; it is a process. The seed is planted, but before the tree can take root and grow and spread it has to be nurtured untiringly by innumerable hands. Our Constitution is yet on the anvil and elected representatives of the people are engaged in making it a true mirror of our live beliefs and our sincere aspirations. To frame a genuine constitution, a people need to scrutinize their own mind and soul very closely. Time-honoured maxims and hallowed principles embodied in a constitution are of little validity, unless a nation feels that it

5

YORK COLLEGE LIBRARY

possesses the spiritual strength to live up to them, unless they echo the voice that is heard unfalteringly in the innermost recesses of its soul. We have earnestly searched our hearts, and though much yet remains to be done, the main features of our Constitution to which we can put our seal with a conscience free of all restraints, doubts or qualms, are to us unequivocally clear.

We have pledged ourselves a Federation with autonomous units, wherein shall be guaranteed fundamental human rights, equality of status and opportunity, and before law, social, economic and political justice, freedom of thought, expression, belief, faith, worship and association.

We have pledged that the Muslims in our State shall be enabled to order their lives in accordance with their faith; but, not forgetful of that perpetual fear of the majority from which Pakistan has delivered millions of Muslims and in humble thanksgiving to God for this deliverance, we have solemnly pledged that our minorities shall enjoy full rights of citizenship and shall freely profess and practise their religions and develop their cultures and that their legitimate interests and the interests of the backward and depressed classes shall be adequately safeguarded.

We have pledged that the State shall exercise its powers and authority through the chosen representatives of the people. In this we have kept steadily before us the principles of democracy, freedom, equality, tolerance and social justice as enunciated by Islam. There is no room here for theocracy, for Islam stands for freedom of conscience, condemns coercion, has no priesthood and abhors the caste system. It believes in the equality of all men and in the right of each individual to enjoy the fruit of his or her effort, enterprise, capacity and skill—provided these be honestly employed. It firmly believes in the right of private ownership, although it frowns on large accumulations of unearned wealth and is greatly concerned over menacing inequalities.

These are articles of faith with us and by them we are irrevocably bound. They are our way of life; and no threat or persuasion, no

6

material peril or ideological allurement can deflect us from the path we have chosen. In proclaiming the objectives of our Constitution, we have called on Almighty God, to Whom alone sovereignty over the entire universe belongs, to bear witness to our resolve and to guide our footsteps "so that the people of Pakistan may prosper and attain their full contribution towards international peace and progress and happiness of mankind."

In our short life as a free nation, we have learned not a little about the world and the times we live in and about ourselves. We have learned that freedom, whether of the individual or of countries, is not everywhere and at all times safe and that the integrity of our own homeland which is dearer to us than our lives will demand of us unceasing vigilance. Our people are deeply distressed at the thought that world-wide destruction might overtake not only the fuller life to which they aspire but the entire human civilization with all its magnificent achievements and illimitable opportunities for good. For youthful countries like ours, which are experiencing but the first pulsations of a free existence, this prospect is profoundly disturbing and not without a touch of irony. We sincerely hope that leaders of world opinion will pursue the path of understanding and will use their wisdom and power to dispel and not to enhance the fears of an apprehensive world. Though freedom has had many births, greed, aggression and intolerance continue, alas, to rear their ugly heads. This is the century of great awakenings in all parts of the globe; and it depends entirely on the leaders of the world whether mankind will awaken to the horrors of darkness or to a glorious dawn.

We have learned much about ourselves, too. Our State began under a number of handicaps, both natural and man-made, and almost before we had time to unfurl the flag to which we now bear allegiance, millions of refugees—the largest number in world history—crossed our borders and sought shelter within our territories. This put us to a test which might have proved disastrous; instead of which our calamities strengthened the determination of our na-

7

tion, and the hard work demanded of us fortified our faith. If the test was to come, we are glad that it came early and when we least expected it. For it gave us the measure of our moral and spiritual resources and even in our immature years filled us with courage for the future that has yet to unfold itself. The task that lies before us is truly immense and we are fully aware of it. We are aware that "liberty does not descend upon a people, a people must raise themselves to it." We are aware that recent centuries of progress and advancement in the world have by-passed us, leaving our resources untapped, our capacities unused and our genius inactive. In all humility but with great faith in our destiny, we the people of Pakistan are resolved to make up for lost centuries within the shortest possible time so that we should never be a source of disquiet to our friends or a temptation to the avaricious. Peace is essential for progress but progress is no less essential for peace. As peace and war today are indivisible, so is progress, and in its name we offer our goodwill to all nations great and small and earnestly ask for theirs.

Vice-President Barkley closed the meeting of the Senate with these appreciative remarks:

On behalf of the Senate, and through it, on behalf of our country, we wish not only to express our appreciation to the distinguished Prime Minister for his visit to us, but also for his constructive and eloquent speech which has just been delivered. We have had many distinguished guests who have addressed the Senate of the United States. I would not wish to draw any comparisons, except to say that no address has been more inspiring, more appreciated, than this one delivered by the new Prime Minister of a new free country. It is an inspiration and a source of encouragement that from the other side of the world has come to us this distinguished representative of democracy and self-government.

The Prime Minister has brought with him a distinguished com-

8

pany, whose names have been inserted in the Record. I cannot present all of them, but there is one in particular whom I should like to mention. We in America, rather belatedly, accorded to women equal rights with men in the processes of government. We learned rather lately that injustice, intolerance, bad government, bad economic and moral conditions affect the home and the guardian of the home and the guardian of the children of the home more acutely probably than these things affect the men. With the distinguished Prime Minister has come his charming, cultured wife, and the Chair should think the Senate would be disappointed—certainly the Chair would—if he did not ask Madame Liaquat Ali Khan to rise in order that the Senate may greet her as the wife of her distinguished husband.

Immediately following his appearance before the Senate, Liaquat Ali Khan spoke to the House of Representatives. He was welcomed by the Honorable Samuel Rayburn of Texas, Speaker of the House, who said—

Members of the House of Representatives, it is my great pleasure, speaking for you, to welcome our distinguished guest to this Chamber, an illustrious citizen in his own country and of the world, the head of a government made up of a great and proud people, an important democracy toward which we feel friendly; we believe its people feel friendly toward us. We trust that throughout the years this good feeling, this friendship, and this cooperation may abide.

It is my high privilege and my great pleasure to present to you the Prime Minister of Pakistan.

Since the Prime Minister's speech largely duplicated his address to the Senate it is not printed here.

FOREIGN RELATIONS: THE INTERESTS OF PAKISTAN IN THE WORLD OUTSIDE

A statesman, well known in history, speaking of his own country, once said that it had no eternal friends and no eternal enemies but that it had eternal interests.

Personally I believe that this is too cynical a view to take of the foreign relations of any country, unless the word "interests" is interpreted very widely. But perhaps for some people it is a good starting point for the study of foreign relations. If I do not adopt it wholeheartedly myself someone else is bound to do so. It might, therefore, be helpful to begin by stating as clearly as I can what the interests of Pakistan are.

To appreciate Pakistan's interests in their true perspective, permit me to recapitulate a page from the recent history of the Indo-Pakistan subcontinent. As you no doubt know, former (that is, British) India was on the 15th of August, 1947, partitioned into two independent sovereign States, namely the present-day India and Pakistan. It is important to remember why this partition came about. It came about because a hundred million Muslims found themselves in a minority in British India and were convinced that under the majority rule of the Hindus their culture was in danger of effacement and their economic position which was low—compared to that of the Hindus, very low—was not only unlikely to rise as rapidly as they desired, but more likely to sink still further. They put forward their irresistible national demand that in those parts of British India where they were in a majority they should be allowed to set up their own State, leaving the rest of British India to the Hindus who were in a majority there. This was agreed to by the

British and by the Hindu leaders; and thus Pakistan, like present-day India, was established as a sovereign State on the 15th of August, 1947.

The aspirations that were at the back of the demand for the creation of Pakistan were, and remain, the strongest urge of the Pakistanis. I cannot stress this point too much because without a full realization of what the Muslims were pursuing when they demanded the separation of Pakistan from the rest of India it would be difficult to understand what Pakistan stands for in the world of today.

Our strongest interests, therefore, are: firstly, the integrity of Pakistan. Having established an independent State after many years of struggle against forces that either would not or could not see any sense in what we regarded as a life-and-death struggle for us, the last thing that the Pakistanis are likely to acquiesce in is that the slightest dent should be made in the territorial integrity of their country.

Secondly, our culture. The majority of the eighty million people of Pakistan are Muslims. Having achieved independence they are determined to pursue the aims for which they sought independence. The most inspiring of these aims is that they should be free to hold their opinions, worship God in freedom and follow the Islamic way of life. The phrase "Islamic way of life" has on many occasions been misinterpreted by some people. It has been misconstrued variously as religious intolerance, theocratic rule, return to mediaevalism and so on. I wish to make it clear, therefore, that we have no theocratic State in mind. We have in mind no special privileges of citizenship for the Muslims in our country and we abhor the idea of applying any religious or cultural coercion to our non-Muslim nationals. But we firmly believe that our religion has taught us certain principles of social and economic justice, and of human values, whose application in statecraft is bound to promote human welfare. Furthermore Islamic belief in the right of private ownership, with Islamic laws and institutions which tend to level down inequalities of wealth, is the best way of tackling economic disequilibrium not

11

only in our own country but everywhere in the world. These are not new beliefs. The Muslims have held them for over thirteen hundred years. We are determined in our country to apply them afresh to the domain of human affairs. Such principles held and practised in the name of religion do not mean intolerance or mediaevalism. Certainly not to our way of thinking. There are certain States in the modern world which though avowedly secular are proud to proclaim that they believe in the Christian way of life and in the pursuit of Christian virtues. They pursue some of the fundamental human values in the name of Christianity. We pursue them in the name of Islam. As followers of Islam, we could not do otherwise.

Thirdly, our desire and our dire need for economic development. I have told you of the basic principles on which we have founded our economic system. Having based it thus we are resolved to use every means in our power and the entire fund of goodwill and co-operation which the rest of the world may choose to offer us, to make up, not for lost years but for lost centuries in trade, in advanced agriculture and advanced industry.

These are our fundamental interests. Given these, any student of international affairs can appreciate our foreign relations and their trends.

Culturally, we feel a natural affiliation with other Muslim countries and our relations with them are of the friendliest. We are keenly interested in the progress and development of the Middle East countries and in the maintenance of their independence, as they are in ours. When I talk of our friendship with the Middle East countries, I do not wish you to infer that I am talking in terms of any power bloc. I am merely talking of the natural and religious links, the common culture and the identity of economic outlook that exist between the people of these countries and our people—links that will stand the strain of many a test and will I am sure prove a stabilizing factor in Asia.

Here I wish to remind you that Pakistan consists of two parts— East Pakistan and West Pakistan—which are about a thousand miles apart. I draw attention to this fact because people are inclined to think of Asia in terms of South East and Middle East and mentally to allot most Asiatic countries to one zone or another. West Pakistan borders on Afghanistan and Iran and has great strategic importance in relation to the oil-bearing areas of the Middle East. But East Pakistan borders on Burma, just about where the Japanese advance was halted during the last war. We have, therefore, vital interests in South East Asia also. Our attitude towards the problems of South East Asia can be explained very simply. As an Asiatic country and moreover one that has achieved independence from colonial rule, we have the greatest sympathy for and understanding of resurgent nationalism in that part of the world. This, as well as the fact that there is a large concentration of Muslims in the United States of Indonesia has, for example, guided our attitude towards the Indonesian Republic throughout. Apart from this we stand for stability in Asia. Above all we want peace in the world not merely as an ultimate aim but equally urgently as an immediate aim. This is an inevitable desire, if you keep in mind the fact that we wish to shed as quickly as possible the inadequacy and the under-development which for centuries have kept our people in poverty, ignorance and ill health. How can we achieve this without stability and peace within and without our borders? The belief is growing in our minds that peace and stability in Asia are essential for peace and stability in the world. We regard with great anxiety any disruptive movement anywhere in Asia which might endanger this stability. It is with these objectives in mind that we have established friendly relations with the Government of the Indonesian Republic and with Premier Thakin Nu's Government in Burma; and we regard the stability of Burma's financial position to be of great importance. We have, as you know, recognized the Central People's Government of China as accepting an established fact and in order to ease the flow of trade. We would welcome a treaty of peace with Japan at an early date and the restoration of Japan's economy.

Europe is farther afield but not without interest to us. We have established diplomatic relations with most European countries and have trade agreements with a number of them. On the colonial questions our stand was made quite clear when the future of ex-Italian Colonies came up for discussion in the United Nations.

Now I turn to our great neighbour, India. Frankly, our relations with India have not been as free from anxiety as we earnestly desire. We have reason to believe that this anxiety is shared by the Indian Government also. I would, however, like to annotate this situation by mentioning two major facts. First that India is a larger country than Pakistan. Second that, whereas some sections in India resented the partition of British India into present-day India—or as they would prefer to be known, Bharat—and Pakistan, and therefore regarded the emergence of Pakistan as a separate State with some mental reservation, at no time either before or after partition has any voice been raised anywhere in Pakistan against present-day India's achievement of sovereignty and of its exercise within its own territory. There are some major matters still in dispute between our two countries. Foremost amongst them is the problem of Kashmir. There is luckily the international agreement between Pakistan and India that the question of Kashmir's accession to India or Pakistan shall be decided by a free and impartial plebiscite of the people of Kashmir. By this we stand; but we have never wished to conceal our anxiety over the inordinate delay that has taken place in holding such a plebiscite and in ensuring, according to the barest requirements of common sense, that the plebiscite when it takes place should be free and truly impartial. Even a cursory study of some of the other disputes will be enough to clarify and justify Pakistan's stand. Take for example the question known as the canals dispute. Nineteen million acres of land in Pakistan are irrigated by canals from five rivers, three of which have their origin in India and the other two in that part of Kashmir which is under Indian military occupation. It is not Pakistan that is in a position to disregard international obligations and neighbourliness in such matters. On the other hand, Pakistan cannot but insist that its international rights

14

should not be disregarded. It is only because our integrity as a State and our international rights seemed to be in jeopardy that, as a self-preservative measure we had to deflect a great deal of our expenditure to the consolidation of our defence.

There is a minority of thirty-five million Muslims in India and similarly a minority of thirteen million non-Muslims in Pakistan. It is a matter of great relief to all concerned that in an agreement very recently concluded between the two Governments, both the Governments of Pakistan and India have solemnly agreed that each shall ensure to the minorities throughout its territory complete equality of citizenship irrespective of religion, a full sense of security in respect of life, culture, property and personal honour, freedom of movement within each country and freedom of occupation, speech and worship subject to law and morality; that members of the minorities shall have equal opportunities with members of the majority community to participate in the public life of their country, to hold political or other office, and to serve in their country's civil and armed forces. Both Governments have also emphasized that the allegiance and loyalty of the minorities are to the State of which they are citizens and that it is to the Government of their own State that they must look for the redress of their grievances. In putting their signature to this agreement, the Government of Pakistan have but underlined a pledge given to the minorities as a basis of the Constitution of Pakistan. We are determined to implement this agreement in letter and spirit, and I believe that the Government of India have the same desire. We realise that a relationship of mutual confidence between our two countries is essential for the peace of Asia and of the world.

Last but not least I turn to the United States of America. I am happy to say that yours was one of the first countries with whom we established friendly and diplomatic relations; it was the first country overseas with which we established trade relations—within a few months of our independence. We look forward to a long period of mutual goodwill and cooperation. If during my visit here we come to a better understanding of each other's point of view, as I am confident we shall, my visit will stand as an event of great importance in the history of Pakistan's foreign relations.

I have only one last remark to make and I will preface it by requesting you to turn your minds once more to what I said earlier about the Islamic way of life which we wish to pursue as an article of irrevocable faith. In a world of conflicting ideologies, nations that have recently achieved full sovereignty are likely to be the victims of mental confusion and consequent instability. Is it not, therefore, a matter of supreme satisfaction that at least one nation amongst such nations should not suffer from such confusion and should as a matter of tradition and belief be pledged to clear-cut and easily intelligible principles of democracy and social and economic justice? That, in our peculiar circumstances, this is the surest ideological safeguard against disruption is amply proved by the fact that Pakistan is one of the few countries in the new Asia whose people are unified and surprisingly free from disintegrating doubts and clashes. In an anxious world this is a good beginning for any State to make. What remains, however, is that we should industrially and economically develop fast enough to implement our own pledges to ourselves within a reasonable time. Unencumbered with ideological confusions, this is the task to which we can address and with the help of God are addressing and will continue to address ourselves. I leave it to you to decide whether this is not the best way in which Pakistan can build itself up as a stabilizing force in Asia. I think your answer will not be very different from ours.

NEW YORK: AMERICA'S METROPOLIS

Your Honour: My wife and I are overwhelmed by the reception you have given us and by the generous words you have spoken. This is my first visit to New York, and indeed to this continent. I was long looking forward to this visit because I wished to see with my own eyes not only the colossal progress that your country has made but what it was that made this rapid progress possible. Already I have seen enough to admire your vigorous spirit of enterprise, your optimistic outlook and the opportunity which your country gives to every individual man or woman to rise to the best of his or her capacities. I am even more impressed by the kindliness and simple affections of your people of which I have received much wonderful proof today. Your city has endeared itself to the world by its great traditions of hospitality and welcome. Of the guests that you have received in the past and will receive in the future, I regard myself as amongst the humblest but also amongst the proudest. You have not only honoured me but, more so, my country Pakistan. May you prosper and by your wide and liberal sympathies continue to bring honour to yourself and to your great nation and country.

Later in the day of 8 May 1950, Liaquat Ali Khan was awarded the honorary degree of Doctor of Laws by Columbia University. Given here is the Prime Minister's citation, read by Provost Grayson L. Kirk of Columbia University to President Dwight D. Eisenhower as a part of this ceremony.

Mr. President: One of the most agreeable features in the life of a great University is the opportunity from time to time to greet eminent guests from other lands. In the course of nearly two centuries of its existence as an institution of higher learning, Columbia thus has been privileged to welcome to Morningside Heights many distinguished men, world leaders in science, letters and public service. In so doing, we believe most sincerely that in our traditional academic fashion we thus help to cement more closely bonds of understanding and friendship among those peoples of the earth who are determined to maintain institutions of democracy and liberty upon which we believe the advancement of civilization ultimately must depend.

Today we are enabled to add one more name to this long and distinguished roster of our guests. His Excellency, the Prime Minister of Pakistan, prepared himself for public life as a student at Exeter College, Oxford. Completing his studies in the law, he was then called to the bar of the Inner Temple in 1922. Subsequently, he returned to India, joined the Muslim League, and became active in political and administrative affairs in his native land. For some fifteen years he was thereafter a member of the United Provinces Legislative Council. Later he was the Deputy Leader, under the late Mr. Jinnah, his friend and colleague, of the Muslim League Party in the Central Legislative Assembly; in 1946 he became an appointed member of the Viceroy's Executive Council.

It was wholly fitting, therefore, that when the separation between India and Pakistan became an accomplished fact in 1947 our guest should have been designated as the Prime Minister of his new country, a post which he has since filled with great distinction and success.

Mr. President, it is, therefore, in recognition of a brilliant career in public service of his people, and as an outstanding leader of a new state whose people have chosen to follow the path of liberty, that I have the honor to present to you for the honorary degree of Doctor of Laws, *honoris causa,* His Excellency Liaquat Ali Khan, Prime Minister of Pakistan. In accordance with our long tradition, may I now read the formal citation for this highest award which the University can confer.

Liaquat Ali Khan, administrator and statesman, now Prime Minister of Pakistan; a graduate of universities in both the East and West, whose youthful study of the law served as a foundation for a career in public life; whose understanding of the hopes and needs of his fellow citizens soon resulted in his becoming a forceful member of their legislative assemblies; whose executive ability was recognized by the late Mr. Jinnah and put to exacting use; whose long political career has not only revealed warm sympathy for the underprivileged, but has included a host of practical measures to improve their lot; and, finally, a man whose ability as a statesman has been tested in his country's struggle for independence among the freedom-loving nations of the world.

The Prime Minister's brief speech at Columbia University, delivered after receipt of his honorary degree, defines in few words the necessities of his new-born state.

PROGRESS AND PEACE: PAKISTAN'S NECESSITIES

Since my arrival in this country it has been my privilege to be the recipient of great honours. The esteem and indeed affection which have been showered on me have been overwhelming, and my heart has been filled with gratitude to the people of your country who have been so spontaneous in their kindness and so generous in their welcome to a visitor from a far-off land.

But there is no honour which I value more or will cherish more in my heart than the honour you have conferred upon me today. For there is no greater honour than this, that those who seek knowledge and truth and place them above all mundane and transient considerations should admit a man to their distinguished company. In honouring me you have done nothing less than this. No human institution can do more.

I am deeply conscious that my merits are not of a measure which should make me deserving of such high esteem. If I could have convinced myself that I, in my own person, had been singled out for the high distinction which you have bestowed upon me, I should have had considerable hesitation in offering myself as the beneficiary of your recognition. But I take courage in the thought that it is not me but my dear country which has prompted your goodwill, and that it is as the servant of my people that you have thought it fit to extend to me the hand of friendship. With this thought in mind, I dare not but bow to your will and for a brief but great moment become a symbol, however unworthy, of my masters—the people of Pakistan. As Liaquat Ali Khan, within the hallowed walls of this

YORK COLLEGE LIBRARY

house of learning, I feel humble. As the servant of my people whose destiny has brought me reflected eminence today, I feel proud . . .

You have accepted me in your midst as the representative of a people who are resolved to uphold democracy and liberty. These words have stirred me deeply. They have reminded me of our way of life, our concepts of social justice and equality, our belief that God is as close to the lowliest amongst us as to the highest—a way of life which we are trying to pursue within the context of our recently achieved independence. They have reminded me of our hard-won liberty and of the vigilance that it will demand of us, in the uneasy and apprehensive world of today.

We are a poor and backward people who but a short three years ago emerged from a long period of suppression to the exhilaration of freedom. In the world around us, however, we find dark forces at work threatening to extinguish the torch of civilisation which liberal institutions such as yours are trying to keep alive. We ask ourselves how a country such as mine whose experience of liberty is so new, so fresh, can take its due share in the advancement of civilisation, when civilisation itself (not in any particular part of the world but over the entire planet which God assigned to the noblest of His creatures) seems to be in dire peril.

The task before a youthful country like Pakistan is how to raise its millions of people from the depths of poverty, ill health and ignorance. This in itself is a gigantic task and a single generation, let alone a single man, can hardly accomplish it. Yet such is the world situation today that in addition to this, we must strive to maintain peace in the rest of the world also, and to persuade those whose power for good or for evil is great and who can influence the future of the world, to use their wisdom to rid mankind of the fear of war.

Progress and peace—this is the double task that seems to have been placed upon our shoulders in this moment of history and although we do not feel perplexed or confused, we are not a little daunted by the immensity of the assignment. Whether the world

22

will be at peace or at war, is in the hands of great nations such as yours. You earnestly desire peace to enjoy the fruits of the great civilisation that you have built up with your energy, your enterprise and your moral qualities. We desire it even more in order to extend the benefits of civilisation to those parts of the world where freedom till a few years ago was only a wish and a longing.

What can we do to help in the maintenance of international peace beyond keeping our own house in order? The answer is not easy to find but when the answer is found we shall not hesitate to follow wherever it may lead us, and we shall not waver.

The conferment, in the name of democracy and liberty, of the great honour which you have bestowed upon me as the representative of my people, I regard on my part as only the reiteration of a pledge, that these nations which strive for peace and progress and the happiness of mankind will find us their friends and that we shall find our friends amongst them . . .

Town Hall of New York and the Foreign Policy Association joined on 8 May in honoring Liaquat Ali Khan at a large dinner. Among the distinguished speakers who preceded the Prime Minister and in a sense introduced him to the gathering were the noted columnist and political commentator Walter Lippmann and Mr. George F. Kennan, State Department authority on foreign relations. Mr. Kennan's speech is printed as the epilogue to this book. Mr. Lippmann's speech follows below.

It is an honor and also a great pleasure for me personally to be allowed to participate in the welcome to the Prime Minister of Pakistan.

Perhaps he will recall the afternoon last November when he was kind enough to receive me in the library of his home in Karachi. I shall always remember it. I was impressed. I was moved. I saw for the first time some light at the end of that long tunnel through which the peoples of Asia are working their way.

23

At the end of the tunnel I saw the dim light of a great hope. At that time, and indeed until less than two months ago no one would have dared to think that it was more than a great hope. It was that the two nations which have emerged in southern Asia—in the Indian subcontinent—would find ways to live together in peace and to become allies and friends and partners, and thus the great center of peace and of order and of progress throughout Asia.

Americans have, I believe, a special reason—and I might almost say a peculiar right—to entertain this hope. With all the differences that exist between us, we have a common experience. Pakistan and India are two nations and states which have emerged as the successors from the partition of the British empire in Asia. Canada and the United States are two nations and states which emerged as the successors from the partition of the British empire in North America. The United States, like Pakistan, is the product of a rebellion which ended in the partition of an empire. Now on that ground, I think we may say with some right and reason that we cannot express our good wishes better or more clearly or more concretely than to say that we hope to see Pakistan and India and Britain as free and as united and as influential in the Indian Ocean and the lands around it as are Canada and the United States and Great Britain in the Atlantic Ocean and in the Atlantic community.

I must confess that a few months ago it was more a matter of faith than of evidence to think that this was possible. Pakistan and India were mobilized. Their armies were drawn up facing each other. Their trade relations had virtually been broken off. On both sides of their frontiers there was talk of war. On both sides of their frontiers there was suspicion fanned into flames by fanatical agitators.

Both governments were new. Neither had nearly enough trained officials to administer a modern state. Both had to face from the day of their independence the immemorial misery of Asia and the relentless pressure of the population against the resources and the means of life.

All that is a long dark tunnel. The light at the end of it was, and is, the character of the two leaders and their immediate advisers and lieutenants, and the great and ennobling tradition which descends to them and to their two nations from Jinnah and from Gandhi, and envelops and guides and purifies their use of the freedom which they have so recently won.

During the past month the light has begun to shine brightly. In the Nehru–Liaquat discussions at Delhi and Karachi the world has seen two statesmen at grips with an ancient, deep, and dangerous religious and ideological conflict. The results already achieved have been remarkable. But what has impressed all who have followed the matter closely is the quality of the statesmanship which these two remarkable men have displayed. They have had the imagination and the audacity to grasp firmly and surely the fundamental issue that divides their countries.

The Pakistanis have feared—and they have had reason for their fears—that if the Hindu fanatics, who assassinated Gandhi, had their way, India would not accept the fact of partition and the independence of Pakistan, and would seize the opportunity to unite the whole subcontinent by force.

On the other hand, the Hindus have feared—and also not without reason, when they watched the fanatic Muslims—that if these fanatics had their way in Pakistan, life would become intolerable for the Hindus.

The fanatics and the extremists on both sides are really dangerous people. It takes moral and personal courage of the very highest order to oppose them.

The two Prime Ministers have faced the fact that until and unless these fanatics are put down there can be no peace, no freedom, and no future for the hundreds of millions of people of the subcontinent, and indeed for all that is left of free Asia.

The foundation of the pact which the two Prime Ministers reached in Delhi, less than a month ago, was a firm commitment by the two governments that each will resist and suppress the ideological and religious fanatics. In plain words, Nehru undertook to deal with the

Hindu fanatics, and the Prime Minister of Pakistan undertook to deal with the Muslim fanatics.

The commitments of this pact rest not only on practical necessity and expediency but on a common declaration of the principle of equality and religious freedom in Pakistan and India. The declaration of this principle is an event of transcendent importance in the history of religious liberty. It is also an event of immense importance in the general history of the modern world. The two Prime Ministers have borne witness before mankind. They have not come to their convictions cheaply and easily. They have come to them through suffering and danger. They have said that for them and for their countrymen there can be no peace except as all men were equally free.

Mr. Prime Minister, we rejoice in your achievements. We are most deeply grateful for the example you are bringing and the lesson you are teaching. It is that when leaders are worthy of their peoples' trust, and when statesmen are equal to their responsibility, peace can still be had with freedom and with honor.

THE RECENT HISTORY AND PRESENT STATE OF PAKISTAN

History has been moving very fast in our century and the political geography of the world has undergone many changes. No new continent has been discovered but familiar continents have had unfamiliar frontiers drawn on them. This has sometimes happened so fast that maps and map-makers have not been able to catch up with the changes.

I should not be surprised, therefore, if some of my listeners, not necessarily in this room, do not quite know where my country, Pakistan, is, although of course I have met an astonishingly large number of people in this country who have a wide international outlook and know as much about events abroad as if they happened next door.

Even at the risk of boring the well-informed people, may I say that Pakistan is a sovereign State of nearly three years of age situated in Asia; that its area is equal to the total area of France, Italy, Belgium and Holland and that eighty million people live in it. Most of them are Muslims.

Three years ago there was in Asia a British India. British India is now no more. What I mean is that it is no longer British. It is in a sense no longer the old India either. For the territory that was known as British India was on the 15th of August 1947 split up into two separate independent countries. Only three-fourths of that territory is now known as India. The rest is Pakistan, the country which I have the honour to represent.

Old British India was partitioned into two countries because there

27

were two major nations living in it—the Hindus who were in a majority and the Muslims who were in a minority although there were about a hundred million of them.

A minority, as you know, always fears the domination of the majority, especially, as was the case with the Hindus and the Muslims, when they have different religions, different cultures, different traditions and different ideologies. When a minority is as big as a hundred million people which is a larger number than most nations in the world, it feels it has the right to have a country of its own. Luckily, in the vast subcontinent in which we lived, there was room enough for two nations. Furthermore, though the Muslims were in a minority in the subcontinent taken as a whole, in certain large parts of it they were in a majority. These are the parts that now constitute Pakistan.

To us the 15th of August, 1947, was a great day. On that day we, the Muslims, had a double sense of freedom—foreign rule had come to an end and we had a country of our own where, without fear of a dominating majority, we could hold our own opinions, worship God in our own way, speak our own language, follow our own customs and pursue our own ideology towards a fuller and richer life.

We began from scratch. In our offices there were few chairs and tables and fewer typewriters. During foreign rule we had remained a backward people except perhaps in the Army where the Muslims had a long soldierly tradition behind them and had won honour for themselves in the two world wars. In other ways, however, we were not up to the mark. Not many of us were traders—fewer still were bankers or technicians or engineers or doctors.

On top of this, as soon as we hoisted our new flag in our new capital, Karachi, two-way mass migration between India and Pakistan started, accompanied by great suffering and heart-rending misery. Within a few months, seven million people crossed over from India into our country to seek shelter. Most of them were poor farmers who when they came over had no work, no land, no tools, no cattle. They were frightened and dazed. Some had not eaten for many days. Many families had lost parents or children on the way, with little hope of recovering them.

For a moment we asked ourselves: Shall we, a new, undeveloped and ill-equipped country, be able to stand this shock? It was a tremendous test of our belief in ourselves. Even our friends were skeptical and shook their heads. We ourselves, I frankly confess, were not a little nervous but our national cohesion and the fortitude and the spirit of self-sacrifice of the common man and the common woman surpassed everyone's expectations. We got together, men and women—yes, women too by the hundred, by the thousand, some of whom had never done a public job before—we got together, we found land, tools and work for the refugees, tended the sick and the wounded, we looked to our harvests, we sent out our students to work amongst the people, we worked without holidays, set up shops, learnt about imports and exports, did everything that we knew, and learnt what we did not know, as far as was possible within the short time—with the single thought in our mind not to go under and not to dishonour the freedom we had so recently won. If I speak of this with some feeling and a certain amount of pride I know that you who love freedom so much will understand and forgive me.

But I will show you the other side of the picture also, for we have a tremendous task ahead of us yet. Pakistan is in the main an agricultural country. Eighty per cent of our people live and work on the land and our methods of agriculture, as in most Asiatic countries, are primitive. We lack education and both our standards of living and our standards of health are low. With industrial advancement and with scientific training we can and must increase the productivity of our land, give our farmer better tools and teach him how to use them, raise his standard of health and education and bring him up to a level of existence which at least does not make him unhappy to compare himself with the more advanced peoples of the world.

Our agriculture is our great asset and our farmers are our great workers. You perhaps know that we are one of the countries that have a favourable trade balance with the dollar area. We have a sound economy. Our budget in each of the three last years has been a balanced budget. We have been careful in our purchases—strictly preferring urgent national necessities to other goods. We produce 75 per cent of the world supply of that little known but much sought after plant, called jute. Some of it comes to the dollar area for making burlap and packing material. Further, we export not only cotton but also wheat; for we are lucky in having surplus food.

Some in this country may ask themselves: How does all this concern us? How does Pakistan matter to the world? Why should we take interest in Pakistan except out of sheer curiosity?

Well, in the first place, in the world of today every country matters or should matter to every other country. The nervous system of the modern world is very sensitive. Nothing seems to happen in one part of the world which has not far-reaching repercussions.

Secondly, Pakistan is in Asia—it is the third most populous country in Asia—and I firmly believe that peace and stability in the world today depend very largely on peace and stability in Asia.

Thirdly, Pakistan like many other countries in Asia is underdeveloped. Whilst you, for example, were developing your science and industry which have given your country the great position it occupies today, we were being ruled by other people. Science and industry passed us by. Our people are poor and backward. Large-scale poverty and backwardness in any part of the world are a menace to peace and civilization. We cannot make up for the backwardness of one or two hundred years sufficiently quickly without the cooperation of the more advanced countries who possess advanced technical knowledge.

When worrying about the development of our country, it did not take us long to come to two conclusions. First, that we must exploit all our resources of land and water to the fullest by putting all our own money and energy into the undertaking and by making the investment of foreign capital easy and mutually profitable. Second, that we shall not be able to get on without taking advantage of the technical knowledge and technical skill of the more advanced countries of the world.

In three brief years, we have pursued these aims sincerely and earnestly and to the greatest extent that the circumstances permitted. We are surveying all our resources as quickly as we can. Our foremost problem is the production of power without which we cannot promote either our agriculture or our industry. We are expanding the capacity of our ports and our communications. We are sending our students abroad for scientific education and technological training and we are utilizing the services of competent foreign experts and consultants.

Of our industrial policy, I hope to have an opportunity, later, in this city, to speak in greater detail. But I would like to say that except for a few specified industries we have thrown open the entire field of investment to private enterprise, and we assure the great pioneers of this and other advanced countries of the warmest welcome and of the greatest goodwill on our part, and we hope we shall have their goodwill and cooperation in return. I am glad to be able to say that right at this moment, the Government of Pakistan is in consultation with the Government of the United States for negotiating a Treaty of Friendship and Commerce which will bring us into greater and mutually profitable contact with the industrialists, manufacturers and businessmen of America, and we have every hope that the outcome will be satisfying. We are also looking forward to the implementation of President Truman's Point IV programme, provided it is suitably followed by and supplemented by private investment from your country, as envisaged by President Truman himself. For we believe that this would be the most courageous, the wisest and the most far-reaching method by which your great country can assure the world of its goodwill and its international outlook and make a memorable contribution to the progress of civilisation in parts of the world where progress is most needed. . . .

Our relations with our neighbour, India, since Partition, have not been free from anxiety—for us, for India, or for our friends all over the world. They have, as you know, been particularly a source of uneasiness to those who realize the great importance of a peaceful and progressive Asia. They have added to the weight of our defense expenditure and deflected our resources from more productive and profitable channels. I am glad to say that as the result of free and frank discussions between me and the Prime Minister of India, we have mutually taken steps to restore confidence in both countries. We have entered into an agreement about our respective minorities and have made at least a beginning in the direction of the resumption of trade between our two countries. I sincerely hope that this will lead to better and better understanding in the future, and desirous as we are of each other's progress, we shall be able to help and promote it in concrete ways. Pakistan has been and will always be ready to settle all differences by negotiation, mediation, arbitration—in fact by all methods of peaceful settlement that can be devised to meet outstanding disputes; but it will never yield to force or coercion in any form. The biggest dispute between us is over Kashmir—the princely state of four million people, 80 per cent of whom are Muslims, which has strong geographical, economic and racial links with Pakistan. Happily there is an international agreement whereby both India and Pakistan are pledged to let the people of Kashmir themselves decide whether they want to join India or Pakistan. We trust that the recent appointment of Sir Owen Dixon by the Security Council of the United Nations, to prepare the ground for the plebiscite, will expedite this plebiscite. We wish him the greatest success in his task and he will certainly have our most willing cooperation.

A question I am sometimes asked is what is the ideology of Pakistan as a State? I will try and tell you this in a few very simple but very clear words. We Muslims believe in God and His supreme sovereignty. In one of the large towns of Pakistan is an educational institution built by some God-fearing people from your country. In the entrance hall is a marble tablet and on it the words "Except the

Lord build the house, they labour in vain that build it." That is exactly what we believe whether we build a house or a State. We believe in democracy, that is, in fundamental human rights including the right of private ownership and the right of the people to be governed by their own freely chosen representatives. We believe in equal citizenship for all whether Muslims or non-Muslims, equality of opportunity, equality before law. We believe that each individual, man or woman, has the right to the fruit of his own labours. Lastly we believe that the fortunate amongst us whether in wealth or knowledge or physical fitness, have a moral responsibility towards those who have been unfortunate. These principles we call the Islamic way of life. You can call them by any name you like.

At present there is no democracy in Asia which is more free and more unified than Pakistan; none so free from moral doubts and from strains between the various sections of the people. But the standards of living of our people must be raised and we must soon equip ourselves to play our rightful part in the modern world, to throw our fullest weight against aggression and towards the maintenance of international peace. That is why we are anxious to develop our resources at the greatest possible speed. For this we need your goodwill and cooperation and the goodwill and cooperation of all the peace-loving nations of the world.

I have spoken to you in English but English, as you know, is not my own language. I wish I could have spoken to you in my own language which is Urdu. Before sitting down allow me to say just two things in Urdu. "Long live Pakistan" and "Long live America." Pakistan Zindabad! Amrika Zindabad!

The following day, 9 May, the Prime Minister and the Begum were guests at a joint meeting of the Far East America Council of Commerce and Industry and the National Foreign Trade Council, held at the Waldorf-Astoria Hotel. Introduced by Mr. Arthur B. Foye, President of the Far East America Council, Liaquat Ali Khan laid out in detail, for the first time in this country, the economic objectives of his country. This speech, if taken with the one delivered 8 May before Town Hall, can be considered to summarize to a large extent the burden of his message to the United States.

THE INDUSTRIAL DEVELOPMENT OF PAKISTAN

I am conscious of the fact that the audience whom I address this evening are not unfamiliar with Pakistan and its problems. Some of them have even visited my country and have exchanged views with our people. My excuse, however, for speaking to you is the hope that in some matters you will find the point of view of Pakistan to be of interest—and the certainty that the contact for which you have provided an opportunity this evening will lead to better understanding and cooperation.

Our country began its career as an independent sovereign nation under a series of handicaps. Before the partition of British India into present-day Bharat and Pakistan, the Muslims, who now constitute the majority in Pakistan, were economically and educationally very backward. On the establishment of Pakistan there was two-way mass migration between Bharat and Pakistan. As a result of this, very great gaps appeared all of a sudden in our economic structure. The trading community which consisted mostly of Hindus was considerably reduced. Most industries and sources of power of British India had been located on the other side of the border. But our trade revived remarkably quickly, due primarily to the energy and patriotic zeal of our people and their determination not to let their

34

newly acquired freedom suffer economic catastrophe; and secondly, to the immigration, into Pakistan, of the Muslim trading community who were driven out of their ancestral homes in India. The quick revival of our import and export trade gave a strong fillip to the internal economy and foreign exchange position of the country. An outstanding feature of the financial position of Pakistan is that for each of the first three years of the country's existence the national budget has been balanced. The State Bank of Pakistan was established within less than a year with a share capital of approximately ten million dollars of which 51 per cent was subscribed by Government. The State Bank manages the currency of the country and forms the backbone of our banking structure. We have also established an Industrial Finance Corporation and a National Bank of Pakistan. The latter is a commercial bank (in which Government has a small share) which will fill the gaps in the banking structure and undertake trading work in the districts on behalf of Government. A Refugees' Finance Corporation with a capital of ten million dollars has also been set up mainly to assist in the economic rehabilitation of refugees in business and cottage industries. The confidence which the balanced budgets and the strong financial position of the Central Government have created within the country is illustrated by the success of the loans floated by Government. A total sum of three hundred million dollars has already been subscribed.

While it is recognised that underdeveloped countries like ours have to march forward on many fronts simultaneously, three items have with us a high priority. They are irrigation, electrification and communications.

Pakistan is predominantly an agricultural country, but our methods of agriculture, as in other Asiatic countries, are primitive. The yield per acre is very low and varies from one sixth to one sixteenth of the yield of various crops in the United States. At present the area under cultivation is about two fifths of the total. We have, however, five major irrigation projects in progress which are planned to increase the area under cultivation by six and one-half million acres. But it is obvious that we could not get the best out of the large expenditure which we have incurred and are incurring on irrigation projects unless we also modernized our methods of agriculture. For this purpose we have under consideration schemes for the purchase of tractors and modern implements, for the manufacture and import of fertilizers, and for cooperative farming to bring modern improvements within the farmer's means. More than half the money allotted to development schemes is earmarked for projects which will help the expansion and modernization of agriculture.

In the field of electric power, Pakistan inherited a total generating capacity which can only be described as meagre. The greater part of this power was generated by old and inefficient diesel and steam stations which had suffered from lack of spare parts during the war and were badly in need of overhaul. The vast possibilities of developing waterpower had been practically untouched. The situation was made worse by the fact that on the partition of British India, the Hindu-controlled managements of electric supply concerns abandoned their undertakings in Pakistan and together with their trained technical personnel crossed the border to the other side. However, within a few months of independence we surveyed our requirements and laid down a target of five hundred thousand kilowatts to be reached in five years. In 1948 we set up a Central Engineering Authority for initiating and pushing forward multipurpose schemes for the control, regulation and utilisation of the water and power resources of the country. We employed foreign consulting engineers of repute to assist the Central Engineering Authority. As a result not only has the deterioration of existing power stations been arrested but there has been positive increase of output. The consulting engineers have now been asked to prepare an all-Pakistan plan for electrical development and to carry out an intensive load survey for that purpose.

The over-all plan will take another six months or so, but in the meantime we are taking measures to relieve power shortage by improving all existing, and constructing new, hydro-electric and thermal stations. Cheap electrical power is the basic need of our country. We are, therefore, doing our utmost to make it available universally, and there is a considerable amount of work already in progress. We expect our hydro-electric power to be doubled by the end of this year and to be quadrupled by the beginning of 1952. Another hydro-electric project is expected to be completed by the end of 1952 and two other projects which are still in the investigation stage, by 1956–57. To supplement these supplies, we also propose to construct central generating stations at appropriate load centres in East and West Pakistan, and are at present surveying for the location of these stations. These projects are aimed at giving us sufficient energy for our industrial requirements, for modernizing our agriculture and for setting up a country-wide network of cottage and small-scale industries which are necessary to supplement the income of our rural population.

We are gradually transforming our system of transport by converting steam engine railways to diesel, in order to be independent of coal as far as possible. At the end of the war, the railway system in East Pakistan had almost broken down because of the heavy strain that it had borne during the war. A good deal of overhaul and repair work has been done and arrangements for the purchase of new broadgauge and metre gauge carriages and of diesel electric locomotives are in hand. Work is also in progress on the port of Chittagong which is the natural port of East Pakistan and whose development is vital to the economic development of that area. In 1947 it could handle only a half-million tons of cargo in a year. Its capacity has already increased to a million and three-quarter tons and will go up to two million by the end of the year. The long term plan which we hope to implement by 1953 provides for additional jetties and wharves and a capacity of three million tons per year. A secondary port is also being developed in East Pakistan, at Khulna.

Industrially Pakistan is backward. In the pre-partition days our potentialities which are not inconsiderable were badly neglected.

We produce 75 per cent of the world's best quality raw jute but have hardly any jute mills. There is an annual production of a million bales of good quality cotton but very few textile mills. There is abundance of hides and skin, wool, sugar cane and tobacco but the industries connected with these were, in the days of the British rule, not located in our part of the sub-continent. In spite of initial handicaps, however, we hope by the end of this year to manufacture one-third of our requirements of cloth and yarn and all our requirements in cigarettes, except high-grade cigarettes, to improve our tanning industry considerably and to be almost self-sufficient in jute-pressing.

Our industrial policy was announced in 1947, and slightly revised in 1948. We have in these statements detailed the measures which we have taken and propose to take in order to create the necessary climate for the investment of private capital in industry in our country. We have thrown open to private enterprise all types of industries with a few exceptions such as railways, posts and telegraphs, armament manufacture and hydel concerns. These few industries, it will be noted, were already nationalized *before* the partition of British India. We have reserved to Government responsibility only for the fixing of targets, the location of industries from the economic and security viewpoints, and the allocation of materials in short supply. Raw materials are now more freely available and the question of allocation of materials generally does not arise. In the matter of location, our aim is to *guide* industrialists rather than to *dictate* to them. The Industrial Finance Corporation that I have already mentioned has a capital of ten million dollars and is to help the development of medium and small industries. A Tariff Board has been set up to give protection to new and growing industries. We have not only halved the import duty on equipment brought into the country from 10 to 5 per cent, but have also given substantial concessions in the matter of depreciation of machinery and buildings, to assist new industries and to enable them to avoid any adverse effects of over-capitalisation due to the high price of capital goods. So far as import duty is concerned, several raw materials are on the free list and we are now examining the extent to which we can further liberalize our policy. In the industrial field left open to private enterprise, we have adopted various measures for encouraging investment. Relief in taxation has been provided for new industries so that profits are taxed after deduction of 5 per cent for the first five years.

The response in our own country has been satisfactory. In the cotton textile industry as well as the jute baling industry our nationals have invested substantially. Some units of textile machinery and some baling presses were imported from the United States. We welcome foreign capital subject to the participation of indigenous capital up to 51 per cent in certain industries and 30 per cent in others *but only if indigenous capital is forthcoming within a reasonable time.* We have also decided to place no restrictions on the transfer of earnings, profits, etc., except those of general application under the exchange control regulations.

We have recently set up an Industrial Development Corporation, charged with the function of promoting certain key industries. As indigenous capital was inadequate and shy and it has taken some time for foreign capital to come forward, we felt that we could not wait and must make a beginning. The main industries within the purview of this Corporation are jute mills, paper mills, fertilizers and ship-building. The Corporation is charged with a five-year target for which it will raise capital in the country and abroad, but Government has made provision to underwrite the capital to the extent that it is not privately forthcoming. These industries will be managed as private industries by Directors who will have, within the limits of national policies, complete freedom from Government interference in manufacture, control and direction. The whole conception and structure of this Corporation is based on private enterprise with such Government help as may be required, the management being left entirely to the administration of the Corporation in association with private enterprise. The maximum extent that Government is prepared to take liability for this purpose is limited to about sixty million dollars, to be spent within the next five years. The first achievement of this Corporation has been the placing of orders for machinery for a number of jute mills, the orders having been financed by the Corporation and private enterprise. Foreign capital would be welcome to associate with the Corporation.

We are most anxious to promote trade between America and Pakistan. All tenders for large Government orders are published in the newspapers in this country and quotations from American firms are treated on the basis of equality with the others. On the question of double taxation, as also for negotiating a Treaty of Friendship and Commerce, we are already in touch with the State Department. The export duty on short-staple Pakistan cottons for which a special market exists in the United States was reduced last year. Pakistan's ability to purchase more American goods depends naturally upon the United States purchasing more of Pakistan's products.

I think I have made it sufficiently clear that we firmly believe in private enterprise over a very large field, welcome the cooperation of foreign investors, and have under active consideration further measures to encourage investment. Considering the great handicaps under which our State started, you will forgive me if I speak of the soundness of our economy with some satisfaction. The fundamental reasons why our economy has withstood all shocks are our inherent economic stability and the unity of our people. We had to divert a substantial portion of our revenue and capital resources to expenditure on defence. But this was mainly because Pakistan did not receive more than a small part of the share of military equipment and stores allotted to it on the partition of the British-India assets, and we had to equip our defence forces almost from zero. This became all the more vital when our relations with India became a source of anxiety. We sincerely hope that increased understanding with our neighbours, of which some happy signs have already appeared, will enable both of us to employ a greater part of our resources for productive purposes. Pakistan has no aggressive designs, no territorial ambitions. But in the uneasy world of today, we feel we must be prepared to resist aggression in all its forms.

I do not need to remind you that there is no democracy in Asia more determined to lead its people along the path of development and progress. We attach the greatest importance to economic and industrial development—mainly through individual initiative, private enterprise and the goodwill and cooperation of free and peaceful nations who have the technical skill and technical knowledge to help in the progress of mankind.

I sincerely believe that prominent among such nations is the American nation. We welcome the authoritative assurance given on behalf of your country not long ago that American capital pursued abroad "its goal of production and recognised its social responsibility to the foreign community in which it operated" and that it did "not desire to dominate but on the contrary proposed to operate within the framework of the social objectives and laws of the foreign country." These are heartening words. They indicate true internationalism.

THE MIDDLE WEST: CHICAGO

On 11 May the Prime Minister of Pakistan arrived in Chicago and was the guest of the Chicago Council on Foreign Relations. Introduced to the Council by Mr. Meyer Kestnbaum, president of the group, Liaquat Ali Khan spoke briefly of Chicago's remarkable growth in the last one hundred years, treating that growth as an inspiration for his own country. He continued by outlining the principal trends discernible in Pakistan's present policy.

PAKISTANI POLICY, DOMESTIC AND FOREIGN

I have recently been trying to educate myself in the history of your fascinating city. A town which began only about a century ago as a frontier out-post of less than a dozen cabins and is to-day the fourth largest city in the world is nothing short of a miracle, and cannot but fill us with admiration. I have read much of the phenomenal development of your commerce and industry which indicated even more than that high degree of initiative, vigour and enterprise which the world has come to associate with your great nation. But when I read that it was in Chicago that Cyrus McCormick's reaper started the entire history of mechanized farming, I could not help wishing that Chicago had been situated in Pakistan. For we are an agricultural country and we want very badly to modernize our agriculture. Only, we need to do it at even a faster rate than Chicago. But who can be faster than Chicago except Chicago itself? . . .

The low economic position which the Muslims occupied in British India was vividly demonstrated when Pakistan started its independent existence. Many of the Hindus of Pakistan abandoned our territories. The vacuum that their departure created in our commercial and industrial life gaped very wide indeed. They were the trad-

44

ers, the exporters and importers, they managed mills and factories and installations, and they engineered them too.

These gaps appeared within a few weeks of the beginning of Pakistan. On top of that, seven million refugees poured over from Bharat into our country. They were mostly poor farmers who had, of course, left their lands behind them and, when they came over to us, were weary, harassed, landless and jobless. It was this double crisis that provided us with the first test of our national resilience. Those days when we had just hoisted our new flag and when we worked on the floors in our offices because we had no desks, will long live in our memory and be an inspiration to us in our coming days. Because, in those days, the common man and woman gritted their teeth and stepped into the breach. Within a short time, we settled our refugees, found jobs for the jobless, revived our trade, built up our banks, stored up foodgrains, and belied the worst fears of the skeptics, both friendly and unfriendly, who had serious doubts about the viability of the new State of Pakistan. The point I wish to make is that what tided us over was neither experience nor skill— for we possessed little of either—but the sheer determination of the people and their intense patriotism. This continues to be our greatest asset and as I hope to be able to show a little later is a very steadying factor in an uncertain part of the world.

The world is becoming growingly conscious of Asia. I have been more than gratified to find the searching interest that American men and women have in the problems of Asia and in the future of Asia. We on our part believe that peace and stability in Asia are essential for peace and stability in the world. Two facts stand out in the Asia of to-day. First, the fact of resurgent nationalism everywhere, impatience with colonialism and, as a legacy from the unhappy past, suspicion of political advances of the western powers. Second, the extreme poverty and backwardness of the Asiatic peoples and their dissatisfaction with their plight. The two taken together form a very disturbing and unsettling mixture. To many they cause mental confusion. People filled with intense national zeal

45

but otherwise beset with moral uncertainty rush hither and thither looking for panaceas, for new ideologies and millenniums over night.

We give thanks to God that amongst these alarums and excursions, Pakistan stands firm. It stands firm because the Muslims who form the majority of its eighty million people have an ideology of their own which we call the Islamic way of life. This is not a new ideology. It is a body of faith, tradition and belief, which has been a part of man's heritage for over thirteen hundred years. We believe that this ideology when applied to statecraft and the conduct of human affairs is bound to promote human welfare. Let me tell you in a few simple and clear words what it is.

There is first the belief in God and His supreme sovereignty. This does not mean either theocracy or medievalism. We do not believe in priesthood or in the caste system. We consider the first to be unnecessary, for God is as close to one human being as to another. We consider the second to be an abomination, for all men are equal. Individual effort and enterprise is the law of life with us as well as the belief that each man or woman is entitled to the fruits of his or her honest endeavor. The pivot of our economic doctrine is the right of private ownership but our laws and institutions have behind them the aim of reducing inequalities of wealth. We believe in democracy, that is to say in the right of people to be governed by their own chosen representatives, in social and economic justice and in equal opportunities for all citizens of whatever race or creed they may be. We do not have to present this ideology to our people as a new manifesto. The principles I have stated are part and parcel of Islam and when we say that we want to follow the Islamic way of life what we mean is that we could not possibly do otherwise. These are the principles that were embodied in the concept of Pakistan when we fought for it.

They are the principles which have helped Pakistan to emerge as the freest of the democracies in Asia and the most unified. As I said earlier, we stand for stability in Asia. We are opposed to aggression in all its forms and we cannot contemplate with equanimity disruptive forces that might jeopardise the peaceful progress and development of the peoples of Asia. . . .

What I have said so far would be enough to show what we stand for in the world and what the trends of our domestic and foreign policies are likely to be. To complete the picture, however, I think I should mention our relations with our neighbouring country Bharat, and also our attitude to the western world. Since the partition, our relations with India have not been free from anxiety. This is a situation that we truly lament. But I would like to remind you of two facts. Firstly, as you would have gathered from my previous remarks, the beginning of Pakistan has not been too easy. Although we have overcome the initial difficulties, we have a long way to go yet, in order to catch up with modern standards of living. For this purpose we have to work hard, to survey all the potentialities of land and water in our country and to make the best use of the power and sustenance that lie hidden there. Peace is therefore essential to us. Secondly, there have always been certain sections of opinion in India which resented the birth of Pakistan. If they accepted it they did so with strong mental reservations. We on our part were glad that Bharat achieved its independence and no one in Pakistan has ever said or thought otherwise. Thus it should be clear that Pakistan is, first and last, interested in the maintenance of its own territorial integrity and of its own international rights. It is not interested nor has it been interested at any time in the past in threatening the sovereign rights of others. Add to this fact that when the assets of British India were divided we were allotted a share of the defence stores which has not yet been fully delivered to us,—and you will see that our expenditure on the consolidation of our defences is not difficult to understand. We sincerely hope that with growing mutual confidence between Bharat and Pakistan, we shall be able to utilize our resources for more productive and progressive purposes. The Governments of Bharat and Pakistan have recently entered into an agreement about the minorities in each country. This agreement has

47

been welcomed by millions of people and if implemented will dispel fear and anxiety on both sides to a considerable extent. Some major disputes will, however, remain; the foremost amongst them being the problem of Kashmir. Although we are confident which way the people of Kashmir, 80 per cent of whom are Muslims, will vote, we will abide by whatever the democratic verdict may be. But more than two years have passed and the date of the plebiscite cannot yet be foreseen. This had sorely tried our patience and as long as things remain in a fluid state it is difficult to check the rising tide of unhappiness and bitterness amongst the people of Pakistan. We have every hope, however, that as the world's understanding of this question increases and Pakistan's point of view is increasingly appreciated, the democratic resolution of this dispute will not be long delayed. Pakistan is prepared at all times to submit all disputes to negotiation, mediation and arbitration: in short, to the most peaceful and most reasonable methods that can be devised.

To the western world we look for two things, that it will maintain world peace and that it will help the underdeveloped countries by throwing open to them the fullest advantages of its experience, its technical knowledge and technical skill. Indeed the two aims are the same. For it is difficult to see how peace can be maintained when there is such glaring economic disequilibrium in the world. And it is difficult to see how this disequilibrium can be removed in time to save the world from the catastrophe of the war, unless the more advanced countries in the world take an elevated and enlightened view of their moral responsibility. We realise that the underdeveloped countries must themselves organise their own initiative and utilize their own resources, material and spiritual, to the fullest. If there are any countries that subscribe to this view but halfheartedly, Pakistan is certainly not among them. Its economy is sound, its successive budgets have been balanced and it has a favourable trade balance with the dollar area. It is fast educating itself, sending its men and women abroad for training and utilizing the help of technical experts from abroad. It is going ahead

48

with practical realistic plans for developing electrical power, for increasing the productivity of its soil and for improving its communications. Its people are full of confidence and possess a degree of unity which is rare among the new nations of the world. But to make up for lost centuries of industrial development is not an easy task, without the goodwill and cooperation of the more advanced and peace-loving countries. Of our industrial policy and of the practical lines on which we invite the cooperation of foreign investors, I spoke not long ago in New York in some detail. We place no restrictions on foreign investments beyond the restrictions of our laws and of our social objectives. The latter comprise the abolition of poverty, ignorance, ill health and technical and economic backwardness. If this were an earlier era, such objectives would put us on one side of the fence and foreign investors on the other. But we live in 1950 and I am speaking in one of the most progressive towns of the United States of America, the country where President Truman's Point IV Programme has been conceived and formulated. Speaking here and now therefore I have no fear, when I ask for your goodwill, that "goodwill" will be merely regarded as a mildly courteous word that no longer means anything. I am confident that men and women of this country who have demonstrated to the world what enterprise and respect for individual effort can achieve for the good of human beings will apply the same principles of freedom and of equal opportunity for all towards solving the problems of those parts of the world which, though distant, are not remote.

MISSOURI: HOME STATE OF A PRESIDENT

After leaving Chicago the Prime Minister and the Begum flew on 13 May to Kansas City where they were welcomed at the Municipal Airport by Mayor William E. Kemp. Like Chicago, Kansas City interested the visitors as a typification of the great central heartland of America. Later on 13 May the Prime Minister was awarded the honorary degree of Doctor of Laws by the University of Kansas City. Chancellor Deane W. Malott of the University greeted Liaquat Ali Khan and conferred the honorary degree upon him with the following citation:

It is nearly 12,000 miles from the heart of our middle west to the new nation of Pakistan.

In this visit of Your Excellency, we recall the beginnings of our own republic one hundred and sixty-three years ago. We had a smaller population, in a more stable era, and in a more isolated day. Yet we are mindful of the aid and encouragement extended by the older countries of Europe to us, as we took the first steps toward our own freedom and our own way of life.

Within the last few months I was privileged to visit Pakistan, and to see at first hand both the grave problems and the great progress this new nation is making along the always difficult road to freedom.

The time has come when the destiny of Asia is in the hands of its own people. To our honored guest today, may I say, particularly on behalf of the nearby state of Kansas and its people, that we have for you every good wish for the future, and in this shrinking globe we are aware that in the destiny of us all we are inseparably bound together in the call for understanding, intelligence and tolerance as we seek together for World Peace.

Student in the ancient halls of the Muslim University at Aligarh in India and of Oxford, and barrister from the Inner Temple defending the rights of people at the bar of justice; thereafter, General Secretary of the All-India Muslim League, member of the Governor

General's Executive Council and first Finance Member in the Cabinet of the Interim Government of India; and now the first in your country's history to be called to the high office of Prime Minister and—following the untimely death of Mohammed Ali Jinnah, father of Pakistan—to serve as the leader of your eighty million people, you, Mr. Prime Minister, have attained the stature and responsibility of world statesman in a decisive moment of history.

In a country which has passed through crisis after crisis since its birth, you have instilled a sense of calm confidence and a vision for the future among your many diverse peoples, whether they be the hardy Pathans from the North West Frontier, who today know peace for the first time in two centuries, or the light-skinned men from the small kingdoms of the Himalayas—Hunza, Swat, Nagar,— or the Sindhi farmers with their wide flowing turbans, or simply the common men and women of your great cities like Karachi, Lahore, and Chittagong. To them and all others you have zealously carried the inspiring purposes of your Constituent Assembly: "democracy, freedom, equality, tolerance and social justice . . . minorities freely to profess and practice their religions and develop their cultures . . . the legitimate interests of backward and depressed classes . . . equality of status, of opportunity, and, before law, social, economic and political justice, and freedom of thought, expression, belief, faith, worship and association"—purposes you are rapidly translating into realities that may well stand as a shining example to all the world.

Into the tragic turmoil that has shaken the great Indo-Pakistan subcontinent almost since the moment of Partition, you have brought strength of energy and perseverance, firmness of character, depth of responsibility, and an unshakable sense of justice—all tempered with a deep humanity. During the dark days of internecine strife— with fanatics inciting wholesale murder and destruction, with mass migrations of millions of people from ancient homes and possessions clinging desperately to life in primitive camps, with great cities scarred by plunder and burning rubble—you, with the Prime Minister of India, moved courageously among the people of your dominions inspiring peace and reason and understanding.

A plain man withal, your thought has been plain and straightforward, your action direct and unequivocal, your purpose to give an ethical content, befitting plain people everywhere, to the pressing political and economic conditions of our day. True son of the people, your devotion to the ideal of one world for all men has been exemplary. You have inspired confidence in your people at home, in the people of the Far East, and in people throughout the world in the practical ideal of democracy.

As a leader of a civilization rich and creative in modern no less than in ancient history, you bring to us today the privilege of conferring upon you this honorary degree, attesting our admiration and affection for your people, and symbolizing the material, intellectual, and spiritual ties that unite our countries in a common fellowship to walk the road of destiny together.

On the recommendation of the Faculty and by virtue of the authority vested in the Board of Trustees, and by them delegated to me, I confer upon you the degree of Doctor of Laws, admitting you to all the rights and privileges pertaining to this degree, in token of which I hand you this diploma, signed and sealed with the seal of the Corporation; and direct that you be invested with the hood appropriate to this degree.

In this speech of 13 May which followed the award of the degree of LL.D. to Liaquat Ali Khan, the Prime Minister restates the strengths and weaknesses, the powers and needs, of his country in terms of the modern world.

PAKISTAN AND THE MODERN WORLD

In conferring a degree upon me you and the University of Kansas City have bestowed upon me and my country an honour for which I cannot adequately thank you.

For my address today I have advisedly chosen the subject of "Pakistan and the Modern World." I have done this for two reasons. In the first place, I am conscious of the fact that you have been kind enough to select me as the recipient of your recognition, in order to do honour to my country rather than to reward *me* for my inadequate merits. It is fitting, therefore, that in expressing gratitude for your generosity, my country more than myself should speak to you on this occasion.

In the second place, we live today in an era of widening horizons. It is in a sense an era in which new countries are being discovered. More than four centuries ago great explorers from Europe voyaging out to discover the continent from which I hail, discovered your great land. You, with your growing interest in the affairs of the world, are poised in a moment of history when you cannot but carry that voyage forward. If I may be permitted to say so, that discovery of Asia has not yet been accomplished. In fact it has only just begun. In speaking to you today, I trust I shall be of some assistance to you in discovering a part of Asia which I know well and which is very dear to me; and in pointing out some of the links that destiny is forging between your people and ours.

Pakistan is a new state; or to be more exact, a new democracy. As a democracy it is not yet three years old. There was a time when your

55

country where the traditions of civil liberty, freedom and democracy have now taken such firm root, was a new and young democracy and the memory of your struggle for independence was yet fresh in the minds of men. If you can, in your imagination, reconstruct those times for a little while, you will in many ways be reading the history of Pakistan and of the first three years of its new life.

Till three years ago, Pakistan was only an ideal and a longing. In the vast subcontinent where present-day Bharat and Pakistan were situated and where the British held sway, there lived a hundred million Muslims who for centuries had made this part of the world their homeland. They lived, side by side with three hundred million others—mostly Hindus who had come to this continent in an earlier era. As the day of freedom for these four hundred million people drew near, it became increasingly obvious that at the end of the British rule the one hundred million Muslims would have to live their new life as a perpetual political minority. Long experience and the history of several centuries had taught them that under a dominating majority of three to one, freedom from British rule would mean to the Muslims not freedom but merely a change of masters.

It was not merely a question of religious differences, as that phrase is generally understood. It was not merely that, whereas the Muslims were monotheists, the Hindus were polytheists, or that the Muslims believed in the prophet of Arabia and in Christ and the prophets of the Old Testament, whereas the Hindus did not. The differences were even more pervasive than this and created a maladjustment between the two peoples in almost every situation of their daily lives. The Hindus believed in a caste system, which made it a sin for those at the top of the hierarchy to eat with the so-called lower human beings or in some cases even to touch them; the Muslims believed in the equality of all men, regarding even priesthood as unnecessary and a negation of the bond which exists between God and each of his creatures. Their economic outlooks were also very different. The Muslims believed in the right of private ownership for every one, whether man or woman, and had laws of inheritance and economic institutions, which unlike those of the Hindus were designed to promote the distribution of wealth and discourage vast unearned accumulations.

But since the Hindus were much larger in number, the Muslims feared that under their domination, the culture of the Muslims would suffer a great setback and would perhaps be totally eclipsed. Furthermore in a country which was on the whole backward, the Muslims, economically and industrially, were even more backward. It seemed certain to them that, as an unalterable and perpetual minority, their economic position would grow even worse. Thus to the Muslims in that part of the world freedom from British rule meant practically nothing unless it meant freedom from the domination of the Hindu majority also.

It was for these reasons that they asked for a country of their own. The demand was not so unreasonable as it was made out to be by some people at the time. The subcontinent was vast enough for two large countries, the Muslims were numerous enough to constitute a nation bigger than most nations in the world, and in the subcontinent there were large enough areas where they were in a majority. It is these areas that were separated and today form the independent sovereign state of Pakistan. We believed then and we believe now that the demand of the Muslims in British India to have a separate state of their own was, both on human and geopolitical grounds, a very reasonable demand. To millions of Muslims it meant the only opportunity for genuine freedom and genuine self-government. To millions of Hindus it gave the same opportunity for developing their own culture, untrammelled by the constant discontent of a large and unmanageable minority. From the point of view of world peace the creation of two independent and comparatively homogeneous states instead of a single uneasy and unwieldy state with great strains and stresses within the body politic was the greatest contribution that could be made towards the creation of a stable new Asia. Peace-loving men and women who today lament the strained relations between Pakistan and Bharat—

57

and none laments them more than we do—should at least have this consolation that had Pakistan not been separated from the rest of British India, far more serious and dangerous cracks would have appeared in that subcontinent resulting in untold upheavals. Potentially, therefore, the creation of Pakistan has by itself dissolved what would have been a perpetual danger zone in Asia.

But it has done more than that. Cast your mind on all the countries of Asia one after another. Almost everywhere you will see intense nationalism, great backwardness, impatience with colonial rule and, in some, a greater or lesser degree of democratic rule. But in many of them you will also see internal strains, moral doubts, ideological conflicts, waverings, hesitations and confusions. Halting democracies and ideological confusions create great anxieties for the governments in Asia, for the peoples of Asia and for peace-loving and world-minded people anywhere. In the midst of these Pakistan stands unified. It stands unified because its people are free from mental confusions which elsewhere create disruption and cast menacing shadows on the future. They have chosen for themselves the part chalked out for them by their simple, practical, clear-cut beliefs and decisions. Foremost amongst those beliefs are the belief in the supreme sovereignty of God, belief in the equality of men, belief in democracy and the right of the people to be governed by their own freely chosen representatives, belief in individual destiny, in the fundamental freedoms of every single man and woman, in the right of every individual to the fruits of his own honest effort, belief in the sanctity of human life and human liberty, belief in the sanctity of the home, belief in universal peace but an equally strong belief in resisting aggression, tyranny and exploitation. We did not have to acquire or inculcate these beliefs after the foundation of our new state. On the contrary, we founded a new state because we wanted to practise these beliefs without being inhibited by the contiguity, and without being thwarted by the domination, of other conflicting ways of life. For us to be undemocratic, or to ignore individual rights whether of property,

58

belief or expression, or to bend our knee to aggression, is to destroy completely the very ideals which inspired us in our demand for Pakistan.

This intensity of purpose and this firm faith have, during the last three years, been demonstrated in ways which surprised our critics and our friends, and in some ways went beyond our own expectations. When British India was partitioned we, the Pakistanis, were asked to set up a new state of eighty million people within a period of two months. We had no capital and no flag. Our administrative machinery had to be built up from scratch. We were allotted an army, but its personnel was dispersed far and wide and could not come together for months. We had no military equipment. Our share of the military equipment of British India which was allotted to us on paper remains largely undelivered even today when three years have elapsed. Being a backward people we had no industry, no engineers and practically no traders. Within a few months of independence seven million homeless refugees driven out of India came over to us in a miserable plight to seek shelter. Had it not been for the unity of our people we might have floundered. But today after three years we are stronger than before. And in spite of some very anxious moments when our international rights and our freedom seemed to be in jeopardy, we are still free.

What are the demands that our freedom makes on us? Our first duty is to ourselves. I do not say this in any spirit of selfishness or chauvinism. A free people must maintain their own freedom first. Otherwise they disgrace the fair name of free men and women all over the world. But the maintenance of freedom requires constant vigilance. "Liberty does not descend upon a people; a people must raise themselves to it. It is a fruit that must be earned before it can be enjoyed." That freedom means freedom only from foreign domination is an outworn idea. It is not merely governments that should be free but the people themselves who should be free; and no freedom has any real value for the common man or woman unless it also means freedom from want, freedom from disease, freedom

59

from ignorance. This is the main task which confronts us if we are to take our rightful place in the modern world. We cannot hold the clock back and therefore it is *we* who must go forward at a double pace, bending all our resources and all our energies to this great purpose. Students of history are aware that during the last two or three centuries of foreign domination our people have not kept pace with the march of civilization. It was during these centuries that western civilization, of which you are the proud torch-bearers, discovered a use for science which, though not new, was so fast in tempo and so vast in its magnitude that it gave civilization a new orientation altogether. This is the phase that for various reasons our people missed. The result is that today we find multitudes emerging as large, free nations in Asia with their material and mental resources utterly undeveloped and with their standards of living so low that the world conscience should not be content to leave them stagnant. Our ancient steadfast faith which is such a source of strength to us on the ideological front in these modern uneasy times must be wedded to the pioneering virility of modern technology. This is the synthesis we must achieve and achieve quickly, not merely for the sake of progress but for the sake of world peace itself.

For I sincerely believe that war and peace and progress and prosperity are all indivisible today. The innumerable millions of Asia, heirs to ancient cultures and ancient civilizations, have, after centuries of suppression, entered upon a new and dynamic phase of nationalism. Most of them were accustomed to looking at the West from the position of subject peoples and could see little beyond the less attractive side of what to them was Western civilization. Their newly won freedom has, however, corrected their vision and they are better able to see both the Western world and their own surroundings in their true perspective. While on the one hand they are filled with admiration at the sight of the progress and the advancement of civilization in such great countries as the United States of America, they are more impatient than ever before with their own misery and backwardness and are keenly searching the horizon for the signs of a bright day. They are acutely aware of the great contrast between their own standard of living and the standards of living in the Western world. This disequilibrium is in many ways most disquieting and has in it the seeds of unpredictable upheavals. For the sake of world peace, for the sake of world civilization Asia must be made stable but it cannot be made stable unless discontent is removed and the germs of disruption are killed by better and cleaner living which means no more and no less than enabling the peoples of Asia to enjoy the fullest advantages of freedom and democracy. In this situation, we consider the role of Pakistan to be that of a stabilizing factor in a backward and discontented part of the world. We hope to be able to play this role successfully by our strong faith in God, in democracy and in our own unity, by the resources of our lands and waters and by our will to work. On these points Pakistan stands firm.

What, however, is the role of the Western world in this situation? It is to demonstrate that true democracy is international in its very conception and does not shirk its responsibility for the maintenance of world peace; that it discharges this responsibility by defying not only this or that particular aggressor, but aggression everywhere; and that it has a constructive and not merely a defiant outlook. We conceive the role of the Western world to be the enlightened one of sharing its great fund of knowledge, skill and experience with those who were denied their opportunities but who constitute a major part of the world's population and without whose progress, the world will limp along only on one leg, if at all. I have met many liberal-minded and thoughtful men in your country to whom these are the only aims worth pursuing in the domain of international affairs today. I am certain therefore that the vast majority of your people regard the emergence of the democracy of Pakistan, its progress and future development, as of great importance in Asia for they are convinced that Pakistan's strength will be a happy augury for peace.

An American statesman pointed out the other day the great similarity of the beginnings of Pakistan with the early days of America; of how America began mainly as an agricultural country just as Pakistan is today and of how both struggled successfully to free themselves of foreign rule. As your belief in individual enterprise and in civil liberties has led you to great heights both as a productive and as a democratic country, so we hope that our country, too, by following the same path and by believing in moral values will shorten the period between its emergence as a peaceful stable democracy and its emergence as a prosperous state—in order that our co-operation with the peace-loving nations of the world, which we are most desirous to promote, should have weight and substance and we should be enabled by preserving our liberty and by uplifting our masses, to make our full contribution to the security and happiness of mankind.

May I leave this thought with you today—this, and the heartfelt gratitude of one whom you have honoured as the servant of a democratic and determined people. By your generous gesture of kindness and esteem, you have almost relieved me of the pleasant task which I came here to perform, namely to bring Pakistan and the United States of America closer together in the name of humanity and world peace.

On the evening of 13 May, after the ceremony at the University of Kansas City, Liaquat Ali Khan addressed a joint dinner meeting of the Chamber of Commerce of Kansas City and the Kansas City Council of World Affairs. His speech, similar to that of 9 May in New York City, is given below in somewhat abridged form in order to avoid exact repetitions from that address.

ECONOMIC AIMS OF PAKISTAN

Earlier today in this town I had occasion to speak of the origin and birth of Pakistan and to describe the conditions which made it necessary for the Muslims of British India to demand the partition of what is now known as the Indo-Pakistan subcontinent into the two independent sovereign states of present-day Bharat and Pakistan. My object in doing so was not merely to reiterate a page of recent history, which by now is sufficiently known to well-informed people all over the world. My object was to try and convey to my audience the determination of the people who achieved what is almost a unique event in history, namely to bring into existence on the map of the world a country which has been significantly described as the largest Muslim, and the fifth most populous, state in the world. If you will permit me, I will carry the story a little further from that point, to reveal certain hard facts which I hope will be of interest to my audience this evening.

When the frontiers were drawn between Pakistan and present-day India, we were faced with a situation fraught with difficulties which at the time looked almost insurmountable. We were asked within a short period of two months to set up administrative machinery (where no such machinery existed before) for the government of eighty million people over an area equal to the area of France, Italy, Belgium and Holland put together. We found that practically none of the major industries or main sources of electrical and other power were located on our side of the border. In our new country, as in the entire subcontinent before the birth of Pakistan, banking, trade and economic life in general, were controlled by the Hindus, who also had amongst them what little technical personnel was available in our part of the world. Soon after partition, these people abandoned our country and, instead, we received from across the border the largest body of refugees known to history— a multitude of seven million people, mostly farmers and mostly poor, who had been driven out of their ancestral homes in the neighbouring dominion.

Thus Pakistan began its economic life under the worst possible conditions. I believe it was some such situation which was envisaged by certain people who had opposed the idea of partition on the ground that the new state of Pakistan would not be a viable state.

Well, only three years have elapsed. Three years are a very short period in the life of a country; and when they happen to be the first three years, they are taken up in preliminaries and are almost negligible. Yet what is the position today? Within these three years our import and export trade revived so quickly that our internal economy and foreign exchange position were rehabilitated with surprising ease. Within less than a year, we had established the State Bank of Pakistan which is the backbone of our banking structure and manages the currency of our country. We set up a Refugees Finance Corporation with a capital of ten million dollars in order to assist our refugees in business and cottage industries. Year after year our budget has been balanced and when government floated loans, their success was phenomenal.

This is a matter of no small pride for us; for by and large our people had very little knowledge and experience of such matters. Once more it was sheer determination, and the sheer will of our people to work and to learn which made this success possible.

If I had time, I could tell you more of this. I could tell you how with a very few trained men we had to train others as far as we could and try to tackle problems that we had never tackled before.

64

It did not take us long to realize in which direction lay the path to progress. We are an agricultural country. Eighty per cent of our people live on the land. Speaking in Kansas City, for whose leading industries agriculture has for many years provided the raw material, I know that I am speaking to people who will give us both their sympathy and understanding. Our methods of agriculture as in most Asiatic countries are considerably out of date. Only two fifths of the land is under cultivation. Our productivity compared to the more advanced countries is very low and the income of our farmers who are the mainstay of our economy is meagre. We are therefore going ahead on a number of irrigation projects, by which we hope before long to bring another six and a half million acres under the plough. But the large expenditure incurred on these will not give us full returns, unless our farmer is equipped with modern tools and modern methods of cultivation and, what is more, is helped by cooperative farming to find such methods and such implements within his means. In the forefront of our industrial development, we, therefore, place the development of cheap electrical power. For that purpose, we have created a central engineering authority for promoting multi-purpose hydro-electrical schemes and have engaged foreign consultants of repute to assist us in preparing an all-Pakistan plan for power development.

Besides this, there are other industries also which are engaging our earnest attention. Under the British rule, our industrial potentialities which are by no means inconsiderable, had hardly been tapped. We produce 75 per cent of the world's best quality of raw jute, but have hardly any jute mills. We produce about a million bales of good quality cotton per year, but have very few textile mills. We have plenty of hides and skins, tobacco, sugar-cane and wool but the industries connected with these were, under the British, not located in our part of the subcontinent. We hope, by the end of this year to . . . improve this situation considerably. As indigenous capital was inadequate and foreign capital has taken some time to come forward we have recently set up an industrial development corporation to which has been assigned the function of promoting certain key industries such as jute mills, paper mills, fertilizers and ship-building. These industries will be managed as private industries by directors, who, within the limits of national policies, will be completely free from government interference in manufacture, control and direction. The Corporation is based on private enterprise with such help as government may be required to give. Such a corporation gives both to national and foreign investors a very high degree of security. Our industrial policy is to throw open to private enterprise all types of industries with a few exceptions, which were already . . . under state control even before the partition of British India. Government has reserved to itself the responsibility only for the fixing of targets, the location of industries and the allocation of materials in short supply. . . . Relief in taxation has been provided for new industries. We welcome foreign capital, subject to the participation of indigenous capital, . . . and we place no restrictions on the transfer of earnings, profits, etc. except those of general application under the exchange control regulations.

I put these facts frankly and clearly before you for we are earnest and sincere in the development of our country and it would not pay us to delude ourselves or others. Our people suffer from poverty, ill-health and ignorance. We are most anxious to take ourselves out of these depths within the shortest possible time. It would not pay us to be lazy. It would not pay us to mince matters. It would not pay us to be uncooperative. We invite your cooperation and the cooperation of all peace-loving and advanced countries of the world provided they love freedom as we do and are aware, as we are, of their moral responsibility in the world of today. We cannot without such international cooperation—not on a one-way but on a two-way basis, on a basis not only of mutual good will but of mutual benefit—we cannot, I say, without international cooperation shed the backwardness and the inadequacy of centuries sufficiently quickly to make our fullest contribution to the cause of world peace in these difficult times. I will never be tired repeating that without peace there can be no progress and without progress there can be no peace. The backwardness of Asiatic peoples is a menace to the peace of the world and it is the moral responsibility of all of us to remove it and thus rid the world of the atmosphere in which discontent and disruption flourish. Peace in the world is difficult to maintain without stability in Asia. To maintain stability in Asia Pakistan with the best goodwill in the world can only go a certain distance and no further—that is to say no further without international cooperation.

What is Pakistan's contribution, you might ask, to stability in Asia? How does it regard its own moral position? . . . Morally and ideologically our position can be very simply stated. The majority of our people are Muslims who believe in God, and in the domain of human affairs follow the Islamic way of life. Some people are alarmed at the mention of God's name in human affairs. They suspect some narrow sectarianism, intolerance, fanaticism, perhaps even theocratic rule. These things are far removed from our conception of the Islamic way of life. On the subject of God I do not think people in the United States of America will misunderstand me. . . . Only today, in the University of Kansas City, a speaker was kind enough to refer to our purpose as "The purpose to give an ethical content, befitting plain people everywhere, to the pressing political and economic conditions of our day." Man cannot sustain himself by material considerations alone. That is why the basis of our constitution is the recognition of God's supreme sovereignty over the universe and the belief that we humans, however high the position in which we are placed, are but the instruments of His will and can only flourish and prosper if we humbly carry out His divine purpose. We firmly believe in democracy and if we did not, it would be utterly in vain for us to have fought for Pakistan. . . . We believe in social justice, and what is social justice? It is to create such economic conditions that should you go out into the street to distribute alms, there should be no one so wretched, so needy and so poor, as to look at you expectantly. We do not believe in levelling down people so as to kill all initiative. We believe in levelling up people so that the humblest amongst us should be happy and contented. This is our ideology and these are the fundamental principles of our economic life. They are articles of faith not only with me and my colleagues in the government but with millions and millions of our people. This is our way of life. This is our religion. No threat and no persuasion can shake these beliefs of ours. In our minds there is no doubt or confusion. We are proud to say that amongst the new nations of the world there is no democracy more free than the democracy of Pakistan and none which is more unified. Poor though we may be, backward though we may be, young and inexperienced though we may be, we are neither poor nor backward nor immature in our love for democracy and for freedom. This is not calculated thought but something that pulsates in our very hearts. That is why I am speaking to you here tonight with the same warmth and same affection with which you have received me amongst you. If you are the "Heart of America" I speak to you from the heart of Pakistan. Bless you all.

THE WEST COAST

Liaquat Ali Khan arrived in San Francisco early in the morning of 16 May. On that day he delivered three major speeches. Two, those given before the Commonwealth Club of San Francisco and the San Francisco Committee on Foreign Relations, are omitted here as repeating largely statements made elsewhere. In the address below, given at the University of California, Berkeley, the Prime Minister challenges the younger generation with problems it must play its part in solving.

QUESTIONS FOR THE WORLD AND FOR AMERICA

Since my arrival in this country nearly a fortnight ago, I have received nothing but hospitality and kindness and affection. I have supped and dined at many a sumptuous table and I have broken bread with many friends in their homes. On most of these occasions your people with their great modesty and with an almost embarrassing willingness to listen to the other man's point of view, have me speak to them and have put to me many questions. Whether I have been able to enlighten them is more than I can tell for I have nothing very profound to say. I am not a wise man of the East. I am a simple man who as the servant of my people has a clear-cut job to perform. Most of almost any day of mine at home is spent silently listening to others.

But in speaking to you today I have a peculiar sense of relaxation, even exhilaration. Long after people of my generation have passed from this world, you of the younger generation will be assessing their work, lamenting their mistakes and, I hope, profiting by them. You will be passing verdicts on us which history will be more likely to endorse than our opinions of ourselves. You have yet a vision which fatigue has not dimmed and decay has not touched. Within the walls of this great house of learning, you pursue truth and knowledge unceasingly and unflinchingly. I come to you today

therefore not with ready-made answers but with questions to ask—
questions that keep stirring in my mind.

I will put these questions before you not on my behalf but on
behalf of my country for it is as the servant of my people that you
have honoured me today with your company and it is as one of the
humble workers of my country that you have sought me out as
worthy of your attention.

In the emergence of Pakistan as a sovereign independent nation,
you have seen a strange and almost unique phenomenon of this or
of any other age. You have seen new frontiers drawn on the map
of Asia with such rapidity that maps and map-makers have not yet
been able to catch up with them. In the subcontinent which till the
15th of August, 1947, was known to the world as British India lived
the Muslims, a hundred million of us, side by side with another
great nation, the Hindus, 300 millions of them—both the inheritors
of ancient cultures. And yet so great was the difference in their outlooks that maladjustments appeared between them not merely in
political life but in almost every situation of their daily lives. As the
day of freedom from foreign domination approached, uneasiness
increased and the Muslims began to wonder whether as a perpetual,
unalterable, political minority in a country of four hundred million
people, freedom from the British rule would really mean freedom
from all suppression; whether in the land to which their forefathers
had come as proud conquerors several centuries ago and to whose
civilization in the domain of civics and aesthetics they had made
such valuable contributions, the future of the Muslims in the face of
a dominating and aggressive majority held any promise of economic
development or of cultural progress. In their anxiety and perplexity
they groped for solutions but found none that could fill them with
optimism.

At this moment, arose a man amongst us who saw farther and
more clearly than any of us, a man who for years had fought the
British side by side with the Hindu patriots but who, more than
any of his companions, sought freedom not for the Hindus alone

71

but for the Hindus *and* for the Muslims. His name was Mohammed Ali Jinnah. All his life he had been a great constitutionalist and a passionate student of democratic institutions. What he said was in its simplicity and truth so startling that for a long time people could not take it in. He said that, in a democracy, a political minority should have the opportunity of converting itself into a majority but if it is so situated that it can never hope to change its minority status, no constitutional safeguards can adequately protect its rights. The three hundred million Hindus of British India are a perpetual majority. The one hundred million Muslims are a perpetual minority. And since vast and unbridgeable differences separate them and in the political life of the country there is no possibility of their ever changing places, democracy in these circumstances would have no real content. He uttered the simple truth that a hundred million Muslims are not a minority; they are a nation, larger than most nations in the world. The vast areas of British India where they were in a majority was their country. Its name was Pakistan—a name which our greatest modern poet had given to it in one of his inspired visions. Mohammed Ali Jinnah's simple and clear truths cleared the atmosphere of cant and doubt and electrified the Muslims from one end of the sub-continent to the other. We called him Quaid-i-Azam, the great leader. He filled the Muslims with his own indomitable determination. He lived to see his dream come true, to see the jubilation of millions of Muslims at the birth of Pakistan—the largest Muslim country in the world and the fifth most populous—to see the green and white flag of Pakistan hoisted over the capital, Karachi. And when he passed away eighty million people of the new nation of which he was the father bowed their heads in sorrow and reverence.

I am often asked the question: true that by dividing British India into Pakistan and present-day India you have saved the majority of the hundred million Muslims from being relegated to the position of an unalterable political minority, but has this division eliminated or effaced minorities from that sub-continent altogether? It is obvious that this has not happened nor was it expected to happen. There is still a minority of thirty-five million Muslims in India and a minority of thirteen million non-Muslims in Pakistan. But between these numbers and a hundred million there is a difference not of quantity but of quality. A minority of a hundred million depressed and discontented Muslims in the vast Indo-Pakistan sub-continent would have been the greatest single unstable element in the world. It is our firm belief that the emergence of Pakistan, where the majority of these Muslims can now lead a life of their own, has saved the architecture of New Asia from a strain which would have been excessive and extremely hazardous for the peace of the world.

None of us in Pakistan since our independence has for a single moment regretted the decision that was taken by our great leader and our people. On the contrary every day that has passed has convinced us that if we had done otherwise, history would not have forgiven us.

From the beginning, we were faced with enormous difficulties. . . . Certain elements in the neighbouring country which had resented the emergence of Pakistan tried to break Pakistan by throwing upon it within the space of a few weeks the economic burden of seven million refugees, who, driven out of their ancestral homes, sought shelter with us. This was attended by retaliation and caused great suffering and misery in both countries. But none of our people even in their greatest moment of pain and anger ever resented or questioned the right of their neighbours' enjoying their own freedom and independence. The two governments, as you know, have recently come to a happy understanding about the humane and just treatment of the minorities in their respective territories. This understanding has been enthusiastically welcomed by every man, woman and child in Pakistan and it shall always be our earnest and proud endeavour to see that democracy and the equality of citizenship irrespective of race, creed or religion which are the fundamental principles of our way of life and to which we have solemnly and before God pledged ourselves in our constitution, are strictly observed. If we fail to observe them, we should have disgraced Pakistan and made a mockery of the very principles for which we fought. . . .

Thus came into existence a new democracy in the world. But if democracy is not merely a word and not just a form, let me ask you what its demands are. Democracy undoubtedly means freedom but does it mean freedom for governments and for the ruling classes; or does it mean the freedom of the common man and common woman? Surely freedom does not mean freedom to govern as you choose, but the freedom to *be* governed as you choose. And how do you think the people of our country would like to be governed? They would, I can tell you, abhor to be members of a society which is atheistic or whose civic life has no ethical content or in which the system of caste prevails and all men and women are not born equal, are not free to exercise individual initiative or to enjoy the fruit of individual effort. But do you not think that they would ask of democracy something more than these? . . . Today we find multitudes in Asia emerging as large free nations but still living in the depths of poverty, ill health and ignorance. Our ancient steadfast faith is a great source of strength to us on the ideological front in these uneasy times, but unless democracy redeems its fundamental pledge to be government *for* the people, it may not be able to stand the strain of the inevitable test that resurgent nationalism in Asia is bound to put it to.

In this situation we consider the role of Pakistan to be that of a stabilizing factor in a backward and discontented part of the world. We hope to be able to play this role successfully by our strong faith in God, in democracy and in our own unity, by the resources of our lands and waters and by our will to work.

Already in the short period of three years we have shown to the world our determination not to go under. In spite of the great shocks that we have received, we have a sound economy. We are enlarging our ports and improving our railways, we are expanding our educational system, we are sending our students abroad for training, we have employed foreign technical consultants, we are planning large-scale electrification, we are bringing more and more land under the plough, we are mechanizing our agriculture and we are improving the lot of the farmer. And here is the first question that I want to ask you: what is it that we could have done in these three years that we have left undone? That is not a rhetorical question. This is a question which we are constantly asking ourselves and whoever gives us a helpful answer will earn the gratitude of a nation.

But I assure you that to make up for lost centuries of technological development is not an easy task without the goodwill and cooperation of the more advanced peace-loving countries. Our people are full of confidence and possess a degree of unity which is rare among the new nations of the world. We realize—not half-heartedly but fully and clearly, that under-developed countries must themselves organize their own initiative and utilize their own resources, material and spiritual, to the fullest. Can we however remove the menacing disequilibrium and the disquieting contrast in the standards of living in the various parts of the world sufficiently quickly to ward off the catastrophe of war unless the whole world and especially the advanced countries of the world treat our backwardness not as a local or a national but as a world problem? I ask you to ponder whether war and peace and progress and prosperity are not all indivisible today or whether peace can be maintained without progress any more than progress can be maintained without peace.

I believe that your people earnestly desire peace. We, who have just begun to live, can hardly wish for annihilation to overtake us when we have not yet taken our first few breaths. What can we do to maintain peace in the world beyond keeping our own house in order? It seems to us in the East that only those who can make war can primarily maintain peace. If they are in earnest about it, is their way not clear?

When we find strong and powerful nations boldly defying aggression, we are heartened by their stand but we ask ourselves two questions: firstly, is aggression to be defied only where we dislike the aggressor or is aggression to be defied in all its forms, big and small, and wherever it may appear? If the first, we will be doing no honour to democracy or justice or freedom but to the principle of biological survival. If the second, we will be serving the cause of freedom everywhere and giving hope to new nations. Secondly, is defiance, however stimulating it may be, enough? Are there not vast fields for constructive effort by which alone can enduring peace be built up?

Yours is a great country with enormous resources of wealth, experience and technical skill. We, who believe in individual initiative, effort and enterprise do not believe that the era of private ownership is over. But we do believe that we have entered upon an era when capital should come out of its shell and move in the spheres of international social objectives and move on from exploitation to production. Your country fought for its own independence once. You have been the great exponents and the jealous guardians of freedom. Words from your declaration of independence and your constitution have inspired men in far-off lands. You have shown to the world what human effort can do for human welfare. You have no colonies and I believe no territorial ambitions. Has not your history therefore equipped you more than most nations to be among the leading architects of the enlightened internationalism of the future? We Asiatics in general and Pakistanis in particular are waiting to see what your answer will be. We do not know what you will say but should you decide that construction is the best way to defy destruction, you will find the people of Pakistan amongst your staunchest friends. I have spoken to you with great candor and from the depth of my heart for we are a simple and frank people as you are; we hold our freedom dear as you do and we love peace, if possible, even more than you do.

Also omitted from this volume as adding nothing to the Prime Minister's expression of his point of view is the speech delivered by him on 17 May at the Fairmont Hotel in San Francisco before the World Affairs Council of Northern California. However, the introduction on that occasion, by Dr. Monroe E. Deutsch, President of the Council and Provost Emeritus of the University of California, is printed as a felicitous statement of the West Coast's welcome to Liaquat Ali Khan and the Begum as individuals and as representatives of their great nation.

The World Affairs Council of Northern California has in the past been honored by the presence of some very distinguished guests. To these we are delighted to add our eminent visitor of today, the Prime Minister of Pakistan, the Honorable Liaquat Ali Khan.

Pakistan is one of the world's youngest nations, one of the world's youngest democracies, but its history goes back to remote times.

Our distinguished speaker has given a demonstration of his earnest belief in the imperative necessity of solving international problems by peaceful means, by discussion and agreement, rather than by force of arms or bombs. The recent agreement between Pakistan and India, reiterating the guarantees of fundamental rights in both nations, does the greatest of credit to the ability and sincerity of the two leaders of these new nations and should serve as a model for the older nations of the world.

Our speaker's career has been a broad and busy one. After nine years as a student in Aligarh College he went to England and earned the degree of Bachelor of Laws at Exeter College, Oxford. After being called to the bar in England, he returned to his native land, becoming advocate in the Punjab high court. He served in the United Provinces Legislative Assembly for fourteen years, subsequently in the Central Legislative Assembly. During that period he also was a member of the Indo-British Trade Delegation to London. Of the Muslim League he has been one of the outstanding leaders. The portfolio of Finance in the interim government of unified India was entrusted to him during 1946-47, and in 1947 on the establishment of an independent Pakistan he was elevated to the eminent post of Prime Minister.

The country in whose government he plays so important a part is indeed a large one, with an estimated population of eighty million persons, the fifth most populous state in the world. It is essentially an agricultural country, though there are a dozen cities with populations exceeding a hundred thousand.

The independence granted Pakistan in 1947 was the result of a forty years' struggle, but it must not be forgotten that by its own choice Pakistan is also a Dominion of the British Commonwealth of Nations.

Pakistan was chosen as the fifty-seventh member of the United Nations.

Such visits as our guest is paying to this country have the two-fold advantage of giving us the opportunity of coming to know him and at the same time furnishing him with a sight of our land and our people.

We are also delighted at the presence of the Begum, whose part in the life of her people has been a noteworthy one. Educator and economist, she has been both the Prime Minister's indefatigable co-worker and a constant source of inspiration to new services on the part of the women of Pakistan.

And, Mr. Premier, may the ties between our nations become increasingly strong and may we side by side strive to maintain peace among the peoples of the world!

I present to you the Honorable Liaquat Ali Khan.

Town Hall of Los Angeles, like New York's Town Hall, welcomed the Prime Minister on his arrival in California's southern metropolis, 18 May 1950. He was introduced by Dr. Arthur G. Coons, President of Town Hall and of Occidental College, and gave the address which is printed here.

PAKISTAN, THE NEW ASIA, AND WORLD PEACE

My wife and I have travelled twelve thousand miles to come to your country, drawn here by the gracious invitation of your President. And we have travelled another three or four thousand miles to come to your great city. On my way across your vast country I have met many of your countrymen. Many people doing many kinds of jobs but all sharing the common characteristics of kindness, frankness, simplicity and hospitality. I have spoken to many of them and they have spoken to me. What is it that we have been saying to each other?

Well, on my part, I confess I have been anxious to talk to them of my country. For although many of the esteemed compatriots of yours who have come to our country have shown an extraordinary understanding of our urges and our problems, we in the centre of Asia have sometimes a feeling that you in the United States of America regard the distance between your country and ours to be much greater than it appears to us from our end.

I have therefore spoken on many occasions of the birth of our nation and of the origin of our State. I have tried in my way to explain what it was that prompted a hundred million Muslims of British India to demand that a country of their own should be carved out for them, out of that vast subcontinent. I have tried to explain that our demand for the partition of British India into two independ-

79

ent sovereign states, namely present-day India and Pakistan, arose out of the conviction that without such partition democracy could not work in our part of the world. . . .

Your people, for their part, have embarrassed me by their more than courteous and more than modest interrogations, and have heartened me by their willingness to listen to our point of view and to understand our approach to our national and international problems. Today you have shown the same courtesy by asking me to speak to you on "Pakistan, the New Asia, and World Peace."

I will try to interpret the facts of the situation in which our country is placed and will try to show their bearing on the questions which are implicitly contained in the title of my talk.

First of all, it is our belief that the birth of Pakistan itself—that is to say the partition of British-India into two independent States—has by the very act made a great, though silent, contribution to the stability of Asia. The two nations that lived together in British India were in their outlook on life so divergent, that to force them into one single unit would have been to expose the new architecture of Asia to excessive strain; for, the divergence between the Hindus and the Muslims has very deep roots. It was not merely a question of a difference in religion. The religion in each case meant a different way of life altogether and affected not merely doctrines and beliefs but the daily lives of millions of people. Although at the time there were many sceptics who regarded the partition of British India to be unnecessary and even fool-hardy, experience has shown that the separation of Pakistan from present-day India has eliminated an epicentre of dangerous upheavals in Asia. . . .

From the positive point of view, the emergence of Pakistan has at one stroke brought into existence, in the very heart of Asia, a political unit of eighty million people most of whom are Muslims and therefore democratic: not as a matter of calculated thought, but as a matter of religious faith, belief and tradition. Democracy is one of the cardinal principles of Islam and is woven into the very fabric of our social life. . . . The enthusiasm and, indeed, passion, with which the Muslims worked for the triumph of this idea, has created a momentum towards the democratic goal which will take a long time to spend itself out although, of course on our part, we are determined that it shall never be exhausted. For if we stray from the democratic way of life in political or in social matters and become apathetic to the principles of the equality of men, the dignity of individual effort and enterprise, equal citizenship and social justice for all, irrespective of race or creed, we shall cease to be the nation that we are, the nation we dreamt to be.

The fact that the majority of our people are Muslims has other important implications.

In the first place, it makes for homogeneity, for Islam is a very simple, clear-cut religion and does not admit of any major variations. This homogeneity has been demonstrated on more than one occasion during the history of the past few years. For example, when the late Mohammed Ali Jinnah of revered memory, the father of our nation whom we called Quaid-i-Azam or the Great Leader, articulated for us our obscure but deep longing for freedom and called it "Pakistan," his clarion call had a lightning effect and within a very short time stirred the heart of a hundred million Muslims from one end of the subcontinent to the other. Again, when the influx into Pakistan of seven million destitute refugees bent us almost double with the enormous economic weight that was placed on the back of our new nation, it was the unity of our people that saved us from collapse. It is the same unity that enables us to take quick and almost unanimous decisions in our national affairs. . . .

In the midst, therefore, of alarums and excursions, Pakistan stands firm, with its steadfast faith in its own ideology, earnestly endeavouring to apply it to the practical world of human affairs, in order to promote the welfare of mankind. This way of life is not a new manifesto that we have presented to ourselves. We have not adopted it because we have emerged as a new nation in the world. We emerged as a new nation because we believed in it. This way of life is not a political creed with us. It is our religion. It is not something that only I or my colleagues in government subscribe to, as a matter of expediency. It is a view of life which is shared by millions and millions of people in our country. And when I say that they believe in it, what I mean is that they could not possibly do otherwise, however strongly the winds of conflicting doctrines may blow around them.

Whilst on the subject of Pakistan in the new Asia, I would also like to draw attention to the geographic and strategic position of our country. I do so because our frontiers were drawn less than three years ago and not all the maps which people carry in their minds have been able to catch up with the change. Pakistan comprises two parts, East and West. Whereas one borders on Burma, not far from where the Japanese advance was halted in the last war, the other borders on Iran and Afghanistan and has an important situation in relation to the communications to and from the oil-bearing areas of the Middle East. This part also controls the mountain passes through which the Indo-Pakistan sub-continent has been invaded ninety times in the past centuries. Most people are inclined mentally to divide the greater part of Asia into South-East Asia and the Middle East and to allot each country to one or the other zone. Because of its peculiar situation, Pakistan is vitally interested in the development of events in both these zones and has, thus, a doubly delicate position.

Pakistan therefore, politically, ideologically and strategically holds a position of great responsibility. I have already spoken of our firm unshakeable belief in democracy. To that I wish to add that we are also determined to defend our freedom, whatever the quarter from which the threat may come. In addition to this, Pakistan is resolved to throw all its weight to help the maintenance of stability in Asia. Stability in Asia is most important to us not only for our own freedom and progress but for the maintenance of world peace. As things appear to us in our part of the world we cannot imagine how world peace can be maintained unless Asia is stabilized.

What can we do, what can the world do, to ensure stability in

Asia? To answer this question it is necessary to have a full realization of the living conditions of millions of people in that continent which contains, as you know, more than half the population of the world—a population moreover which is not apathetic to, or isolated from, the main currents of the world. The great fact of Asia is the poverty, ignorance and ill health of its people. The low standards of living which obtain there are a menace to world peace and cannot be viewed with equanimity or ignored with impunity.

It is the moral responsibility of every democratic government in the East to organize all its resources and all its energies to the great purpose of uplifting its people from the depths in which they live, if such an existence as they lead can be called living. I have told you of the extremely favourable circumstances which already exist in Pakistan for the development of the democratic idea but we are fully aware of the fact that the freedom we value so much is of little use to the common man and the common woman unless their living conditions can be improved at least to such an extent that when comparing themselves to people of the more advanced countries of the world, they do not feel bitter and unhappy.

To this end we are doing the utmost that we can. Even in the midst of all our troubles and our handicaps, we are earnestly and sincerely going ahead with plans for expansion and modernization of our agriculture (which is the mainstay of our economy), with the development of electrical power to help both agriculture and industry, and with creating the necessary climate for the investment of indigenous and foreign capital in industrial concerns with the social objective of production and development. The basis of discontent in Asia as well as of the various theories for a speedy removal of the misery of the people, is economic. It is by its efforts in this field that a government which claims to be democratic, or in other words, claims to be government for the people, should be judged. I am glad, therefore, to be able to say that the economy of Pakistan is sound. Our economic policies have created such confidence amongst the people that when government floated loans

83

even in the days of the greatest difficulties with which our country was beset, the success of such loans was phenomenal.

But in the task of the economic rehabilitation of the people, Pakistan, like most Asiatic countries, can only go a certain distance and no further—that is to say, no further without international cooperation. The question that we should all ask ourselves is: can Pakistan make up for the lost centuries of technological advance and industrial development sufficiently quickly to give weight and substance to its contribution to world peace? The clear answer is that without international cooperation few countries by themselves can today discharge their responsibility as effectively and as quickly as they may desire. So far as the prospects of an immediate world war are concerned it will be nothing new or profound if I were to say that it is not the people in Asia who can pronounce upon it with authority. Our responsibility is to keep our own house in order, to go ahead with the enormous task in front of us, of developing our resources, of educating our people and of demonstrating to them in actual practice the benefits of democracy. Whoever helps us in promoting these aims will help us to help peace.

Since we strongly believe in the importance of stability in Asia I would like, if you will permit me, to say a few words about our relations with our neighbor, India.

It is a well-known fact that since independence, our relations have not been easy. We have had to incur a considerable amount of expenditure on the consolidation of our defense. We wish we did not have to do this and could have deflected all our resources to more productive channels but in order to see this expenditure in its true light, I would like to remind you of the fact that the bulk of the share of military equipment that was allotted to us on the partition of British-India has been refused to us. We therefore had to equip our army almost from zero. We have no aggressive designs, no territorial ambitions. In fact, whereas in India there have been and probably still are, certain elements who resented the emergence of Pakistan as an independent nation, never has a single voice ever been

84

THE PRESIDENT'S WELCOME

AT HYDE PARK WITH MRS. ROOSEVELT

AT A NURSERY SCHOOL

AT A FACTORY

raised in Pakistan against India's full right to enjoy its sovereignty and independence within its own territories. Recently, an agreement has been entered into between the governments of Pakistan and India on the subject of the treatment of minorities in each country. This has removed anxiety from the hearts of millions of people and, if fully implemented, will go a long way towards easing tension. Some major disputes between ourselves and India, however, remain—the chief amongst them being the problem of Kashmir. Culturally, economically, geographically and strategically, Kashmir—80 per cent of whose people like the majority of people in Pakistan are Muslims—is, in fact, an integral part of Pakistan. The bulk of the population of Kashmir are at present under Indian military occupation. There is an international agreement between India and Pakistan that a free and impartial plebiscite shall be held in Kashmir to let the people of Kashmir decide for themselves whether they would like to join one or the other of the two countries. But—and this is our main grievance—two years have elapsed and the date of the plebiscite is not yet within sight. On all disputed matters, on which no agreement may have been arrived at, Pakistan has been willing to arrive at a peaceful and just settlement through negotiation or mediation or, failing both, through arbitration. The conduct of the Government of Pakistan over the many differences of opinion that arose in the passage of the Kashmir dispute through the Security Council of the United Nations, is ample proof of what I have said. But to force or coercion, we shall never submit.

If I have been able to convey to you the strong urge for self-government, self-development, democracy, freedom and liberty among the people of Pakistan which achieved the unique phenomenon of creating on the map of Asia a new State of eighty million people, it will not be difficult for you to infer that we passionately desire peace in order to accomplish that for which we founded our country. You, I sincerely believe, desire peace too. But whereas you desire it in order to continue to enjoy the fruits of the great civilization which you have built up with your vigour, your enterprise, your initiative, your love of liberty and your other great moral qualities, we desire it in order to have the barest chance to translate some of our dreams into reality. For you it would be a great pity, if, God forbid, you should fail in your laudable aim. For us it would be a situation full both of pity and irony if annihilation overtook us along with the rest of the world when we were experiencing but the first pulsations of a free life. We know that you are determined to defy aggression and we hope that you will make no distinction between one aggressor and another. But we also hope that you will not regard defiance as enough, but will build up world peace more firmly and more securely in the vast constructive fields that are open to you with your experience and your technical knowledge. In such a task, you will find Pakistan amongst your friends.

Later on 18 May, Liaquat Ali Khan was guest of honor at a dinner given in Beverly Hills by members of the film industry. He was introduced by Mr. Y. Frank Freeman, President of the Motion Picture Association, and in reply gave the following brief talk concerning the concepts of independence and interdependence.

A DECLARATION OF WORLD INTERDE-PENDENCE

You have been a free people for one hundred seventy-four years. Pakistan has had freedom and independence for only thirty-three months. But freedom is an ageless inheritance, and I hope that we and all the peace-loving free countries of the world shall always stand together, differing in age perhaps, but never differing in our common devotion to the cause of freedom.

The Pakistanis have been significantly described as the fifth largest nation in the world. With a stable government, a balanced national budget and a people united on the principles of democracy, freedom, equality, tolerance and social justice, Pakistan extends its hand in friendship to the freedom-loving peoples of the world.

The words of your great heroes who wrote your Declaration of Independence and your Constitution have been quoted by freedom-loving individuals and peoples in many parts of the world. But it is now high time that the world had another Declaration not superseding the Declaration of Independence but expanding it, not abrogating the sovereignty which free peoples have won for themselves with hardship, toil and blood, but expressing the equally valid and equally noble fact of the interdependence of men and nations in the modern world. The size of the world shrinks year by year. The only way to keep pace with it is not by shrinking our minds and hearts but by enlarging them. Enlarging our minds to know and understand the people who live outside our own frontiers. Enlarging our hearts to appreciate beneath all differences of language and culture,—the common humanity, the common destiny and the aspirations for freedom that should make us all one.

A few days ago, I stood before the simple brick tomb at Mount Vernon and placed a wreath there—the tribute of my country to the father of yours. I stood on the porch of the house there—overlooking the broad lawn that sweeps gracefully down to the Potomac—and I tried to think the thoughts which must have been in George Washington's mind when he stood there—when the United States was a young republic—as Pakistan is today, testing its new-fledged wings in an uncertain world. And I knew for certain that he must have thought what the father of our nation, the Quaid-i-Azam, the Great Leader, Mohammed Ali Jinnah thought when his great dream was realized and new vistas of the destiny of the eighty million people of his nation opened before his eyes.

You have fulfilled George Washington's dreams in your own way. All the way across the United States I have seen the great monuments to your spirit of enterprise and tonight I am in Hollywood. Actually I am in Beverly Hills, I understand. But Hollywood is here for Hollywood has now become more than a place. It is a great industry, a centre of many arts and a world institution. And Hollywood holds in its hands one of the most powerful keys to the enlargement of the mind and heart which the world now needs more than ever before in its history.

You can if you wish, write, on strips of celluloid, the Declaration of World Interdependence. Your stars shine as brightly in Karachi and Chittagong, in my country, as they do in Kansas City or Chattanooga in yours. Through the medium of films, you are acquainting the rest of the world with America and through the same medium, America is becoming better acquainted with the rest of the world. I am sure you are aware of your tremendous responsibility, as you are aware of the impact you have and the influence you exercise by your appearance on millions of screens in the world. When you openly air your problems, whether through motion pictures, or through the press and the radio, you can render a service to freedom and liberty all over the world. If your great nation can openly face

88

and openly discuss its problems, you offer a noble example to others in the family of nations.

I am not talking about propaganda. I am talking of the dissemination of truth and knowledge and understanding. Your films are good ambassadors to the extent that they are true to their primary mission of entertainment and true reflection of American life. As such we welcome them, as links in the strong bond of mutual understanding, goodwill and cooperation which—I should like to think—my visit to the United States and your country's most generous welcome have helped to forge.

And now my visit to the United States will in a few days be drawing to a close. What will I take back with me to Pakistan? A host of memories of a great, kind and hospitable people, a people who have fulfilled their own dreams and yet are not above self-criticism. We have our dreams too and we hope we also have your quality of self-criticism. We hope we shall meet the challenge of reality as you met it two centuries ago. You have made the limitations of reality starting points for new advances. We aspire, in our own way, to do the same. In 1776 you were a young, predominantly agricultural republic as Pakistan is today. North America then seemed, and was, much more remote from the rest of the civilized world than our country is today. The stars and stripes of your flag symbolize the federal unions of your varied states. The green and white fields of the flag of my country represent our different culture groups, enjoying equal rights and equal opportunities as members of the united people of Pakistan. We have much therefore in common and we look forward to a long period of friendship.

In forging that friendship, you here in the motion picture capital of the world have an essential and noble part to play. I wish you success from the depth of my heart.

On 19 May, introduced by Mayor Fletcher Bowron of Los Angeles, the Prime Minister spoke before the Chamber of Commerce of Los Angeles. His speech is omitted here since the subject matter is covered in other texts given in full.

THE SOUTH

Leaving Los Angeles, the Prime Minister and the Begum swung east and south to Houston, Texas, where they arrived on 22 May. There, at a dinner given by the Foreign Trade Committee of the Houston Chamber of Commerce in the famous Rice Hotel, he was introduced by Mayor Oscar Halcombe. In the speech that followed, Liaquat Ali Khan repeated to a considerable extent the economic data given in his address of 9 May in New York. The Houston speech, therefore, appears below in much abridged form.

WORLD PEACE THROUGH WORLD TRADE

Houston has done me great service by adopting for its slogan this year: "World peace through world trade—dollars spent abroad always come home." Your international good sense and your grasp of one of the most essential solutions of the many world problems that face us today could not be demonstrated better than by this fact that I, representing eighty million people in the distant heart of Asia, should arrive here to find you proclaiming the very thoughts that are present to my mind. If I were so bold and presumptuous as to try and give you a message from the under-developed countries of the world, I could not word it more aptly than you have done yourself.

All that remains for me to do on this occasion, therefore, is first of all to thank you for your cordial welcome and your hospitality; secondly to pay you the homage of my admiration for your vigour, enterprise and vision which have achieved for your town a remarkably high position not only in the United States of America but in the world and to convey to you the very best wishes of my country for an even more successful future; and thirdly to tell you of the measures we have adopted and are adopting in order to promote international goodwill and cooperation in the important fields of trade and industry.

Speaking in Texas I have no doubt in my mind that I will have both your sympathy and your understanding. Your State and its men took a noble part in the development of this country and I am confident therefore that I do not have to talk to you at any great length of how we in Pakistan value our freedom and our democratic way of life more than our lives and are determined that within the shortest possible time the benefits that both you and I believe are the benefits of democracy and of a society which believes in individual effort and individual enterprise, should within the shortest possible time be available to the common man and common woman in our country in tangible ways. Pakistan is young. Texas too is young in many respects. We too are trying to diversify our economy and raise our standard of living. We both have certain definite responsibilities in world trade. Pakistan is the prime producer of jute, the essential import of many nations of the world and therefore occupies a position comparable to that of Texas in the case of sulphur and petroleum. . . .

Ever since I have come to America I have met many people who believe that to continue to buy American goods it is essential that the resources of the world must be more broadly distributed, not by exploitation but by stimulating the entire economies of the underdeveloped countries, by enabling them to develop their natural resources and by sharing with them the vast experience and technical knowledge which has made your country's economy so strong. In other words capital must take, in the world of today, a more enlightened view of its responsibility and of its potentialities for good than it has hitherto been constrained to do. We do not preach that the profit motive be abandoned. For the sake of world peace and world equilibrium we only suggest that the profit motive should be combined with international social objectives. I cannot do better than repeat to you the heartening words of President Truman's famous Point IV: "We must embark on a bold new programme for making the benefits of our scientific advances and industrial progress available for the improvement and growth of underdeveloped

93

areas . . . I believe that we should make available to peace-loving people the benefits of our store of technical knowledge in order to help them realize their aspirations for a better life. And, in cooperation with other nations, we should foster capital investments in areas needing development." This is practical internationalism. This is the surest way to build up lasting peace. As one peace-loving democracy to another, Pakistan extends to you the hand of goodwill and cooperation. May success attend your efforts and ours.

*From Houston the Prime Minister and the Begum flew to New
Orleans where, on 23 May, Liaquat Ali Khan addressed a joint
dinner meeting of the New Orleans Citizens' Committee and the
New Orleans Branch of the Foreign Policy Association. The
dinner, at the Roosevelt Hotel, was presided over by Lloyd J.
Cobb, President of International House. In his speech to this
group, the Prime Minister emphasized the essential peacefulness
of his country and of his visit to the United States. His remarks
appear in considerably abridged form since they derive to some
extent from the ideas expressed in his Town Hall address of
8 May in New York.*

MINE IS A MISSION OF PEACE

Since my arrival here I have already visited eight cities in your vast
land and have exchanged views with hundreds of friends. What I
have appreciated most of all in your vigorous and alert country,
second only to your hospitality, is your spirit of enquiry. The United
States of America has been known as the Land of Promise, the Land
of Opportunity. But I shall remember it most as the Land of Hospitality and the Land of Interrogation. One of the many questions
that I have been asked is: "What is the purpose of your visit to the
United States of America?"

Well, in the first place, I am here because of the kind invitation
of your President. But for the magnetism of his welcome, I might
have found it difficult to be tempted to leave my country when there
is a great deal of work to be done there.

If, however, I were asked to assign a purpose to my visit, I should
like to say that my visit is a mission of peace.

Please do not misunderstand me. I do not mean that there are
any differences between our two countries that need to be ironed out.
On the contrary, since the birth of Pakistan our relations have been
more than friendly as that word is understood in diplomatic jargon
and we are looking forward to a long period of cordial relations.

95

But what I do mean is that I have come here to try and understand the world situation, to find our own true bearing in it and to understand more clearly, if possible, what we in Pakistan can do and suggest, to maintain peace in the world.

I have therefore taken it upon myself to tell such listeners, as may care to hear me, in the first place what we regard our own duty to be in this matter and, in the second place, what hopes, we, in the East, entertain so far as the other countries of the world and specially the more advanced countries of the world are concerned, for lessening the chances of conflict and for helping forward the cause of peace and progress.

Permit me, first, therefore to speak about my own country. Pakistan, as you know, came into existence as a sovereign state on 15 August 1947. The territories that we now know as Pakistan were, before that date, part of British India. The four hundred million people of British India consisted, mostly, of one hundred million Muslims and three hundred million non-Muslims, mostly Hindus. Since these two nations differed from each other in ways that affected their daily lives throughout, it was not possible for them to achieve that cohesion which alone constitutes a nation. Their religions were, of course, different but so were their cultures, their traditions, their social and legal codes and their economic outlooks. The Hindus, for example, believe in the caste system according to which some human beings are born superior to others and cannot have any social relations with those in the lower castes or with those who are not Hindus. They cannot marry them or eat with them or even touch them without being polluted. The Muslims abhor the caste system, as they are a democratic people and believe in the equality of men and equal opportunities for all, do not consider a priesthood necessary, and have economic laws and institutions which recognize the right of private ownership and yet are designed to promote the distribution of wealth and to put healthy checks on vast unearned accumulations. A perpetual minority as large as one hundred million would have been the negation of democracy. And so the Hindus and the Muslims decided to part and divide British India into two independent sovereign states, instead of trying to keep it as one large unwieldy state constantly exposed to strains and stresses within it. One of these two states is Pakistan and the other is present-day India, or, to call it by its new name, Bharat.

Our demand for a country of our own had, as you see, a strong democratic urge behind it. The emergence of Pakistan itself was therefore the triumph of a democratic idea. It enabled at one stroke a democratic nation of eighty million people to find a place of its own in Asia, where now they can worship God in freedom and pursue their own way of life uninhibited by the domination or the influence of ways and beliefs that are alien or antagonistic to their genius.

The majority of the eighty million Pakistanis are Muslims. They asked for, and achieved, an independent country of their own because they passionately believed in a certain way of life. Our ideals are, therefore, quite clear to us. . . .

They do not spell out a sectarian, medieval, intolerant, theocratic society. We believe in God and His supreme sovereignty because we believe that civic life must have an ethical content and a higher purpose, which we cannot but conceive of as the fulfillment of the Divine will. But democracy, social justice, equality of opportunity, equality before the law of all citizens, irrespective of race or creed, are also articles of faith with us as are the inalienable right of the people to be governed by their own chosen representatives, the right of the individual to the fruits of his honest endeavours and economic justice which according to our conception does not mean levelling down people so much as levelling up people, not in killing incentive or initiative but forever widening the range of opportunity for all. . . .

In speaking before the Far East America Council of Commerce and Industry and the National Foreign Trade Council in New York I made a full statement about our industrial policy and I will therefore not reiterate the details here. Suffice it to say on this occasion

97

that we have thrown open to private enterprise all industries except a very few which were state-controlled even before the partition of British India, that we welcome foreign capital on a mutually profitable basis and that to encourage industry we have adopted several measures such as the reduction of import duty on equipment, placing several raw materials on the free import list, relief in taxation for new industries, etc., etc., and that we place no restriction on the transfer of earnings, profits, etc., except those of general application under Exchange Control Regulations.

Let me now revert to my mission of peace. The greatest threat to the peace of the world would be instability in Asia. It is our firm conviction that unless Asia is stabilized, world peace is not possible. And the greatest fact of Asia is the backwardness and poverty of the people and the mental confusion and doubts which arise in the mind of multitudes who have become politically free but are poor and ignorant.

In the midst of these disquieting circumstances, Pakistan with its religious belief in democracy and with the unity of its people—so rare amongst the new nations of Asia—stands firm as the most stabilizing factor in an uneasy continent. The basis of discontent in Asia as well as of the various remedies suggested for its removal is economic. It is by the efforts in this field that the democratic governments of Asia will in the last analysis be judged. I have told you of the efforts that we have been able to make during these three years, in spite of our handicaps and difficulties. But in the task of the economic rehabilitation of the people we can only go a certain distance and no further—that is to say no further without international cooperation. Our responsibility for peace lies in keeping our own house in order, in going ahead with the enormous task in front of us, of developing our resources, of educating our people and of demonstrating to them in actual practice the benefits of democracy. But can we make up for the loss of centuries of technological advance and industrialization sufficiently quickly to give weight and substance to our contribution to world peace? The answer is that we cannot by ourselves—few countries can by themselves—discharge this great responsibility as effectively and as vigorously as is necessary, without international cooperation and without enlightened internationalism. The resources of the world must be more broadly distributed by stimulating the entire economies of the underdeveloped countries, by equipping such countries to develop their natural resources and by sharing with them the technical knowledge and the experience of the more advanced countries—and not by exploitation, for this century is a century of great awakenings and I sincerely hope and believe that exploitation is now twice accursed—blighting him that gives and him that takes. . . .

International cooperation without exploitation, to our mind, is the most efficacious and far-reaching programme that the world can follow today in order to save itself from the horrors of war and perhaps of total destruction. In the pursuit of this aim we ask you to bless our efforts as we shall bless yours.

WESLEYAN COLLEGE
LIBRARY
MACON GA.

YORK STATE AND NEW ENGLAND

One day after his New Orleans speech, on 24 May, Liaquat Ali Khan was introduced to the Chamber of Commerce in Schenectady, New York, by Mayor Owen M. Begley. The Prime Minister had now seen many of America's great cities and much of the great expanse of the land. In his Schenectady speech of 24 May he begins briefly to assess what he has seen in terms of what America may mean to the world, while continuing to explain his own country to Americans. Much of the latter material is omitted as already covered elsewhere.

LIVING STANDARDS IN ASIA: AMERICA'S OPPORTUNITY

My wife and I arrived in your great country exactly twenty-one days ago, drawn here by the gracious invitation of your President and by the fame of your land and your people—the land where human effort has achieved so much for human welfare—and the people who have achieved this by their vigorous enterprise, and by following the traditions of individual endeavor and the rule of equal opportunities for all.

I am glad we came, for I have seen a great deal here that has stimulated and heartened me. I have also learned a great deal which has clarified to me the place my country occupies in the world picture.

Pakistan is a new State; or to be more exact, a new democracy. In your country the traditions of civil liberty and freedom and democracy are now firmly established. But there was a time when you too were a new and young nation and the memory of your struggle for independence was still fresh in the minds of your people. What you felt then, is what we are feeling now, except of course that the world situation is quite different now. In two centuries, the world has gone forward and young nations today have passions and anxieties and responsibilities which the young nations of yesterday did not have. . . .

Eighty million people rejoiced when our new green and white flag was unfurled over our new capital, Karachi. We were happy at the thought that we were at last now able to worship God in freedom and to follow our own way of life. For we believe in God and His supreme sovereignty. And our way of life is democratic, politically and socially. Our religion teaches us not to believe in castes, to regard all men as equal, to let each man enjoy the fruits of his honest labour, to believe in social justice and equality before the law for all its citizens, and believes in the right of private ownership. We had now the chance to put all this into practice without being suppressed by a dominating majority of three to one and without the fear that our culture will be eclipsed by other cultures alien to it.

But you must not imagine, when we had an independent country of our own, that everything was laid on for us. On the contrary. From British India we inherited no industry worth the name, no great sources of power, no technical experience or technical skill. We did not inherit any administrative machinery either. We had to set up from scratch and within two months the vast government machinery that was required for the fifth largest nation in the world and for a territory that was spread far and wide. . . .

The great American nation has always been a jealous guardian of freedom. You cannot be unaware of the fact that the low standards of living of the Asiatic peoples are a menace to stability in Asia and that without stability in Asia the world could only have precarious peace. Your great moral qualities and your glorious history fit you more than most nations to build up the internationalism of the future and to step out into those vast constructive fields which are open to you in the underdeveloped parts of the world, constructive fields in which alone the foundations of a lasting peace can be laid. If you undertake this noble task, we are with you, and may God bless your efforts and ours.

From Schenectady to Boston and Cambridge and thence to Canada. At the Massachusetts Institute of Technology in Cambridge, on 26 May, Liaquat Ali Khan made his last major address in the United States. In this final address he returns to the ideas briefly sketched out in Schenectady, expanding them into a well-rounded statement of gratitude to America for hospitality and past help and of hope in America for future constructive leadership toward peace.

AMERICA AND WORLD PEACE

I am glad to find myself at last in the great institution whose fame first reached me many years ago. The Massachusetts Institute of Technology is, to my mind, more than a great institution. It is a symbol of the age. By reflecting some of the best and most significant aspects of American civilisation, it is already influencing the future not only of your own country but, because of its international outlook and sympathies, of lands beyond your own frontiers too. Many have heard of M.I.T. who may not perhaps have yet heard of the Statue of Liberty or the Grand Canyon. I sincerely hope that by producing the type of broad-minded leadership which the M.I.T., I know, is aiming at, you will, directly and indirectly, promote the enlightened internationalism of tomorrow, in the realisation of which the United States of America has, I feel, a great part to play.

Pakistan in whose name you have honoured and welcomed me today is a new country not yet three years old. One should not be surprised therefore to find that besides those in this country—and there are many of them—who take an up-to-date interest in events abroad, there are yet large numbers to whom the new shape of the Indo-Pakistan sub-continent is not clear. As a servant and spokesman of my country, it has been my pleasant task, during my three weeks' visit to this country, to tell them, whenever I had the chance, that British India is now no more, that even present India is only a part of the old British India, and that the rest is now the independent sovereign State of Pakistan, and has been so since the memorable 15th of August, 1947, when Pakistan's green and white flag was hoisted over its new capital, Karachi.

I found others who knew this but remembered only vaguely why the partition of British India into the two sovereign States of present-day India and Pakistan had taken place. It was again my pleasant duty to remind them that the partition had taken place on the irresistible demand of a hundred million Muslims who had been convinced that without such partition democracy could not work in our part of the world.

I further explained that the Muslims who formed the majority of the eighty million people of Pakistan were determined to run their new country according to the Muslim way of life which indeed had been the main reason for their struggle, under the leadership of our Quaid-i-Azam, our Great Leader, the late Mohammed Ali Jinnah, to achieve independence; and that to the Pakistanis, democracy, the right of private ownership and the conception of individual effort, individual freedom and the equality of citizenship and opportunity for all, irrespective of race or creed, were matters of faith, religion and ancient tradition, rather than newly acquired political creeds.

In this way I thought I would help the people of the United States of America to discover Pakistan. For I was sure they would be glad to know and realize that a free democracy—and moreover one which was more free and more unified than most democracies in Asia—had been born in the heart of that continent—with one part bordering on Burma, the other on Iran and Afghanistan, and thus with vital interests in both South-East Asia and in the Middle East.

These were all plain historical and geographical facts. What I really hoped to add to the American understanding of our bearings in the world situation was by conveying, if I could, the proud feeling of our people that politically, ideologically and strategically, their country's position in the modern world was one of great responsibility. I have told you of our religious faith in democracy, a faith which we know will stand many a severe test. But I wish to add that we

105

YORK COLLEGE LIBRARY

are also determined, firstly, to defend our freedom whatever the quarter from which it may be threatened and, secondly, to throw all our weight to help the maintenance of stability in Asia. For, we regard the stability of Asia essential for our own freedom and progress and for world peace; and firmly believe that if Asia is allowed to stagnate and fester, the whole world will be perilously pushed to the brink of unpredictable upheavals.

Asia is disturbed. Mighty winds are blowing across its expanses and strong currents of doubt and discontent swell beneath its surface. In the midst of these strains and stresses we regard Pakistan's role to be that of a stabilizing factor in an uneasy part of the world.

How can we fulfill this role adequately and efficiently?

Before we answer this question let me remind you of the miserable living conditions of millions of people in a continent which contains more than half the population of the world and where young and virile nationalism and the unhappiness and recklessness born of poverty, are creating moral confusions and unsettling thoughts. The great fact of Asia is the poverty of its people. The low standards of living, or rather existence, which obtain there are a menace to world peace. They cannot be ignored with impunity and no one with any political sagacity can view them with equanimity.

The first responsibility for remedying this is obviously that of the Asiatic democracies themselves; and it is by their initiative and their efforts in the economic field that they must judge themselves and the world will judge them. Nowhere in the entire Asiatic continent are the circumstances for the development of the democratic idea more favourable than in Pakistan, but we are fully conscious of the fact that unless the living conditions of the people are speedily improved and the benefits of democracy are demonstrated and made real to the common man and woman in their daily lives, freedom would have little value for them and instead of growing to a full, rich and robust life would begin to gasp for breath.

With this end in view, we are organizing all our resources to the utmost of our capacity and competence. In spite of all our troubles and handicaps, both natural and man-made, we are earnestly and sincerely going ahead with plans for the development of our agriculture and industry, and with creating the necessary climate for the investment of indigenous and foreign capital in industrial concerns, with the social objective of production and development.

With our steadfast faith in God and our democratic way of life, by developing the wealth of our lands and waters, with the unity and strength of our eighty million men and women, with the belief that our liberty is worth more than our lives, and with the determination to resist all threats to our territorial integrity and our freedom of belief, we are striving to make our today better than our yesterdays and our tomorrows better than today, in order to render our due share in promoting the welfare of mankind.

But we have been out of step with the march of civilisation for at least two centuries. Is it an easy task, do you think, to make up for lost centuries in a few years or even a few decades?

No, it is not easy. Before everything else we must have peace. We need it even more badly and desire it even more passionately than you do. For we are just at the beginning of a new life and have barely stepped across the threshold of freedom.

But immediate peace in the world does not depend on anything that we in Asia can do. Immediate peace depends only on those who can make immediate war. We in Asia can only hope and pray that the leaders of world opinion will use their power and wisdom not to add to the fears of an apprehensive world but to dispel those fears. We are resolved, nevertheless, to make the greatest contribution we can, in our circumstances, to the maintenance of world peace; and we know that our responsibility in this respect is to keep our own house in order and to go ahead with the enormous task ahead of us, of developing our resources and educating our people. This is a long task but how else without international cooperation can we give greater weight and substance to our contribution?

Without international cooperation there are few countries in the world that can substantially contribute to peace. Certainly no underdeveloped country can. And yet it is in the under-developed countries more than others that disruption, discontent, strife, and instability are most likely to find a fertile field.

My three weeks' visit to the United States of America has very nearly drawn to a close. Three weeks is a short period to spend in a country so large and so humming with activity as yours. Nevertheless it is my good fortune that in this short period I have been able to avail myself of the lavish hospitality of the American people from coast to coast and to exchange views with executives, dignitaries, civic leaders, magnates, newspapermen, educators, analysts, farmers and children. Everywhere I have found the utmost courtesy and kindness for which my heart is full of gratitude.

This was my first visit to this great country. There are few national workers anywhere in the world who do not know a great deal of the United States of America and of its greatness. A first visit therefore is full of experiences which are no more than an endorsement of the pictures that the mind had already built up before arrival. These one accepts without surprise though not without wonder.

But as one begins to feel the true essence of American life, one feels an exhilaration far beyond anything that the mind could have rehearsed before.

To speak of American enterprise, vigour and love of freedom is to speak of a combination of qualities which has long been a synonym for Americanism. What, however, I have learnt to admire in these few days even more than these, is that quality of the American character which makes the Americans both sensible and sentimental, both adventurous and home-loving, both courteous and direct, both hard-headed and the world's greatest philanthropists. I have been heartened at the wide-spread curiosity about international affairs and at the large number of groups and associations of American men and women who are earnestly studying other people and other countries and who go out of their way to understand them.

But I have been amazed at the capacity of the Americans to question themselves and their own actions. This is a new and most refreshing symptom of greatness in the modern age. In the past it has been the habit of great powers, whether autocratic or democratic, to regard their strength and their position as complete guarantee for the validity of their thoughts, words and deeds. It is true that in this mid-century all powers great and small are flood-lit and stand in full view of the world. This alone could not, however, account for the searching analysis to which the American people are constantly subjecting their national policies at home and abroad. It could not but be due to some great moral robustness which is part of their national genius. It is this American habit of curiosity, analysis and discussion which encouraged me more and more, as my tour progressed, to tell the American people of my country, my people and our problems and to ask my listeners to tell me how our two democracies could cooperate to maintain peace and progress in the world.

My wife and I have been extremely happy here. Your people have showered on us honour and esteem far beyond our merit, and more hospitality and affection than can be the rightful due of any guest. For this and much more we are grateful to the American nation from the depth of our hearts. Pakistan and the United States of America have always been friends; and I hope that the future will unfold itself in ways which will also make them comrades, in the noble task of maintaining peace and in translating the great constructive dreams of democracy into reality.

Because my heart goes out to the people of America, I would like to share with them all my innermost feelings—my hopes as well as my anxieties. I have seen much here that will long live in my memory. You have illimitable resources both mental and material and you are harnessing them at breath-taking pace. You have the greatest store-house of human and natural resources that the world has seen. And yet at times I have felt a little depressed. At others I have felt a little apprehensive. Looking at this great country and then thinking of countries like my own, I have been painfully conscious of the disequilibrium that exists in the world today, a disequilibrium that perhaps an average American cannot realize, for it would be next to impossible for him even to conceive of the poverty that exists elsewhere in the world, of the millions and millions of half-starved men and women and half-dead children who crawl on God's earth in far-off lands.

As I let myself ponder over this, I suddenly see the United States of America as an island—a fabulously prosperous island, where God has showered His plenty—but, nevertheless, an island. And round this island I see the unhealthy sea of misery, poverty, and squalor in which millions of human beings are trying to keep their heads above water. At such moments, I fear for this great nation as one fears for a dear friend.

With monotonous reiteration during my days in America I have appealed for international cooperation. Some may have thought that I was asking for charity. I do not ask for charity. I only ask for the help of the more experienced countries of the world to put our own men to work and to make our own resources yield their wealth. I do so, not for the sake of my own country alone, but also for the sake of America, for the sake of the world. Democracy in the world today cannot remain isolated and flourish. It must go ahead and spread itself or else it will wither away. Prosperity too cannot remain isolated. It, too, must go ahead and spread itself, or else it cannot go on gaining strength. Poverty is pestilence. A man however well-fed cannot remain healthy for long in a pestilential climate and none of us can escape the effects of the world climate for long.

I abhor exploitation and would consider it poor response to the great kindness and hospitality that I have been shown here, if I were to exploit this kindness even for my country's sake. Whenever I have talked of international cooperation, I have always asked that it be scrutinized very closely both as a joint moral undertaking and as a mutually profitable concern. If I did not firmly believe that no democratic country in the world, however great, can get on for long without realising its responsibility to itself through its responsibility to others, I would be false to myself. And if I had not tried to express this, even at the risk of being misunderstood, I should have been false to my host country and ungrateful to the American people, to whom I am beholden for so much.

The question that I would like to leave for the great American people to ponder over is whether the time has not come for them boldly to take democracy to its logical international conclusion; with their resources, their great experience and their technical knowledge to be among the leading architects of this internationalism; and to step out into the vast constructive fields which are open to them in the world and where alone the foundations of a lasting peace can be laid.

Their past history has equipped them to play this role. The future never had any fears for them but has always been a challenge to their indomitable spirit of enterprise and has always beckoned to them with its promise of a better world. Let us all play our part in discovering this new world, where prosperity may be secure, where peace and freedom may dwell unmolested, and aggression and aggressors may be reduced to the position of unpleasant but harmless anomalies.

CANADA, SISTER DOMINION

On 31 May, just twenty-eight days after his greeting by President Truman at the National Airport in Washington, Liaquat Ali Khan addressed the Canadian Houses of Parliament in joint session in the House of Commons Chamber in Ottawa. Prime Minister L. S. St. Laurent welcomed Liaquat Ali Khan warmly and enthusiastically:

In welcoming you today, sir, we wish to pay a tribute to your great country, which in so short a time has attained a place of prominence in the world community; to the rank it holds in the concert of nations as an active member of the United Nations and a sister nation of the Commonwealth, and, last but not least, to the record of your personal achievement as Prime Minister of Pakistan.

We in turn are honoured by your presence in this House of Commons. These words of greeting are naturally addressed to you on behalf of the whole population of Canada; I find it particularly fitting, however, that this welcome be extended to you in our own House of Commons, the centre of the political life of Canada and the very heart of our democratic institutions. It is fitting indeed that greetings from one democracy to another originate in the House of Commons chamber.

The accomplishments of your country since it began its separate political existence on August 15, 1947, evoke sincere admiration. Your countrymen had a long tradition of history in the Asian subcontinent. Still, it is only less than three years ago—and what are three years in the life of a nation?—that the dominion of Pakistan came into being. The astonishing progress made during such a short time augurs well for the future, and you may rest assured, sir, that we in this country will watch your future achievements with the same friendly interest we have had in what has already been accomplished in so short a time.

The future of Pakistan, notwithstanding differences in religion and language, in customs and habits, notwithstanding lands and oceans which separate it from Canada, is closely related to our own through our common association in the United Nations, our partnership in the Commonwealth, and, most of all, in our common belief in those values which form the very basis of democratic life. We hope therefore that our association will become closer and closer as we get to know each other better. The exchange of high commissioners between our two countries is but a first step in this direction.

At present Canadians are wont to associate particularly the names of two men with Pakistan: that of Mr. Mohammed Ali Jinnah, who is regarded as the father of his country and whose name has been immortalized by a grateful people's use of the title "the Great Leader," and your own, Mr. Prime Minister. Mr. Jinnah, in creating a new nation, relied heavily upon you, Mr. Liaquat Ali Khan, whom he described as his "right-hand man." As his death occurred so soon after the establishment of the independence of Pakistan, there fell upon your shoulders, sir, the tremendous task of giving substance to the blueprint of building the machinery of government in order that your nation might effectively express the will of the Pakistan people to contribute through democratic processes to the welfare of mankind.

Mr. Prime Minister, your stay in Canada, though short, will allow you, I hope, to realize the interest we take in your country and your people. As our contacts become closer and more frequent, we shall better understand our mutual problems and be in a position to find a more satisfactory solution.

I wish to assure you that you may count on the understanding and good will of the whole Canadian people as Canada will expect the same from your fellow citizens.

In greeting you on this occasion, may I be permitted, Mr. Prime Minister, to state how happy we are that you are accompanied by your charming wife. Her gentleness and gracious manner almost belie the dominating force which the Begum Liaquat Ali Khan is known to exercise in organizing the women of Pakistan to meet the challenge of providing social security under most difficult circumstances.

On behalf of the parliament and people of Canada I ask that the Honourable Liaquat Ali Khan convey to the people of Pakistan, on his return, our best wishes for their well-being and happiness, together with the assurance of deep friendship.

Members of the houses of parliament, I present to you the Prime Minister of Pakistan.

The Prime Minister of Pakistan's first speech in Canada, follow-
ing Mr. St. Laurent's introduction, summarizes the high points in
his own nation's recent history; but here, he speaks as it were "in
the family" and continues by stressing the immanent values in
the Commonwealth.

PAKISTAN, THE COMMONWEALTH AND THE FUTURE

In permitting me to address you here today within these walls, you have conferred upon me great honour and privilege which I value very highly and for which in the name of my country and my nation I thank you.

As the recipient of this signal token of your esteem my thoughts at this moment turn to the struggle which made it possible for our people to emerge as a free democratic nation to take their rightful place amongst the free nations of the world. For in honouring me today you honour them, their freedom, and the memory of that courageous man who guided their footsteps towards the goal of liberty. You will pardon me, therefore, if on this memorable occasion I am reminded of the father of our nation and the founder of our freedom, our Great Leader, our Quaid-i-Azam, Mohammed Ali Jinnah, of revered memory, without whose vision, determination and burning honesty Pakistan might have remained a vague longing and a distant dream, and the reality, of which my humble presence in your august company today is but a symbol, might never have been born. A sincere patriot, a passionate follower of the democratic idea, and a man who saw farther and more clearly than his fellows, he led the Muslims of British India out of their perplexities and frustrations into the open air of freedom, and gave shape, significance and direction to their quest for liberty. All his life he fought for freedom but since he fought for the substance and not for the shadow, for the thing and not for the word, he let no illusions or catch-phrases obscure his penetrating insight or confound his grasp of the essentials. He struggled long and hard to forge the diverse peoples of his subcontinent into a mighty nation. But foremost as he was in the ranks of those who fought for independence, he was also the first to perceive the inexorable logic of facts, and when the time came, to proclaim fearlessly that the people of British India, bound together though they were in their common subjection, were not one, but two nations, and that to relegate one hundred million Muslims to the position of a perpetual political minority and to force the Hindu nation and the Muslim nation into a single unwieldy state would be the negation of democracy and would create the greatest single unstable area in the world. The great truth that he uttered was so startling in its simplicity that for a long time even some of his close friends and companions found it stimulating, but strange. But the hundred million suppressed Muslims knew instinctively that what he said merely gave coherence and dynamism to their own hesitant inarticulate feelings. When on the 15th of August, 1947, our flag was unfurled in Karachi, a nation of eighty million people thanked God that the Quaid-i-Azam had lived to see his dream come true. And when he left us to rest in God, to whose greater glory he had dedicated himself, we knew that he had bequeathed to us a great destiny to fulfil. Wherever the flag of Pakistan may fly, its capital shall always be that hallowed piece of earth where he lies buried.

The three years that have elapsed brought with them many a trial that we expected and many others that we did not. The mass migration that took place between our country and our neighbour, and caused much unhappiness to people on either side of the border, was a great shock to our economy and a great strain on our administrative machinery, which, it will be recalled, had had to be set up within a period of two months for a population of eighty million and for a territory that was spread far and wide. But our experiences, whether grave or stimulating, only convinced us that the historic decision that the Muslims of British India had taken, to work for a state of their own, was eminently justified. What is more, the events of these early years and the manner in which the people of Pakistan faced them, have filled us with hope and confidence for the future. It was not the maturity of our administration or any previous experience or preparation that helped us to tide over the almost insurmountable difficulties that appeared in our way. Experience or preparedness we had none; for there had been no time for these. It was the fortitude and the determination and the self-sacrifice of the common man and woman which came to our rescue and gave our young state a momentum which will not be easily exhausted and which we believe will grow in strength. No new state could have been launched on its career under greater handicaps. But these three years of struggle have made us a wiser and more unified nation than we could have otherwise hoped to become within such a short time. Although they demanded great courage, patience and vigilance, they have endeared our freedom to us even more and have shown to us very clearly the path to a bright future.

To what use do the Muslims who form the majority of the people of Pakistan propose to put their freedom? This is a question which we as a nation have pointedly asked ourselves and to which we have a clear and unhesitating answer.

First, we are determined that the Muslims in our State shall be enabled to order their lives in accordance with their faith; that at the same time our minorities shall enjoy full rights of citizenship and shall freely profess and practise their religions and develop their cultures, and that their legitimate interests and the interests of the backward and depressed classes shall be adequately safeguarded.

Second, we are pledged to the principles of democracy, freedom, equality, tolerance and social justice as enunciated by Islam. This does not mean theocracy; for Islam does not believe either in priesthood or in the caste system. On the contrary our conception of democracy is possibly even more comprehensive than that which is contained in the institutions of universal franchise and majority rule. For it embraces social and economic justice, the right of private ownership, of each individual to enjoy the fruit of his honest labour—and yet with laws and institutions designed to eliminate destitution and to place healthy checks on vast accumulations of unearned wealth.

All this we call the Islamic way of life and pursue it because as Muslims we could not follow any other ideology or seek guidance from any other source but God, whose injunctions we believe these to be. To abandon these principles would be for us to destroy, instead of create, what we hope to build up and for which we demanded independence and freedom and a separate state.

Third, we are resolved to safeguard our freedom at all costs, whatever the threat and whatever the quarter from which aggression may face us. For our own part we have no aggressive designs and consider it our moral responsibility to pursue the path of peace and to help in the maintenance of peace and stability everywhere, particularly in the uneasy continent of Asia, on whose future, according to our way of thinking, world peace very largely depends. Nowhere in Asia are the circumstances for the development of the democratic idea more naturally favourable than they are in Pakistan; for nowhere are people more unified and more determined to apply their moral concepts of equality and social and economic justice to promote human welfare and to resist any attempt to tamper with their beliefs. But democracy, in Pakistan or elsewhere, is of little use to the common man unless its advantages are made available to him in his daily life and his standard of living is raised at least to a level which gives him a substantial stake in the way of life which he has chosen for himself.

We are fully conscious of this, and consider it our foremost duty to develop the resources of our country at the greatest possible speed. Even in the days of our greatest anxieties we were able to go ahead with this task, and though much remains to be done we are glad that we have been able to revive our trade, to plan for the development of our irrigation, the expansion and modernization of our agriculture and the utilization of our power resources; to keep our budgets balanced and to throw the gates wide open to private enterprise in our industrial development. For this task there is nothing more essential to us and nothing that we could or do desire more passionately than peace.

I know that in Canada I am among friends and speaking to people who are in the same family circle as Pakistan. I feel therefore that I can speak somewhat more intimately than is perhaps usual on formal occasions. Your great country and our young state both belong to the Commonwealth of Nations. I am not one of those who would demand that the bond which exists between the various members of the Commonwealth be minutely defined. It is enough for me to know that they all basically have the same constitution, even though one of them may be a monarchy and another a republic, and all subscribe to the common principles of democracy, freedom and peace. In the uneasy, apprehensive world of today, such a large group of nations with so much identity in their declared aims should be a heartening spectacle to mankind. No practical person would therefore wish wantonly for its disintegration.

Two facts, however, I would humbly and respectfully commend to your attention. First, that with the growth of three Asiatic members of the Commonwealth to the status of dominions, the notion that the Commonwealth ties are mainly religious, historical or racial must be regarded as having outlived its use. If the Commonwealth does nothing more than give the world a lead in establishing the brotherhood of man, irrespective of race, creed or colour, it will still have made a notable contribution to the cause of human welfare. Second, that since the greatest fear of the world is the fear of war, under whose shadow progress alters its aims and millions of humble men and women wait helplessly and apprehensively for an undeserved doom, the Commonwealth has great opportunities for raising the hopes of mankind by outlawing war and aggression and the use of coercion or force as a method of settling disputes amongst its own members. We sincerely believe that in this way this free association of free nations can set the world an inspiring example and can give greater reality and efficacy not only to itself but also to the charter of the United Nations, to whose aims we are all pledged and whose success we all pray for.

The ideals of a freedom-loving, democratic, but young and under-developed, country such as ours could be epitomized in three words —peace, progress and cooperation. These three are but aspects of the same fundamental urge; for there can be no progress without peace, no peace without progress and the removal of the economic dis-equilibrium so apparent in Asia, which keeps more than half the world in poverty and the ferment of discontent, or without inter-national cooperation, which we believe to be the greatest need of all countries, great and small. In the pursuit of democratic ideals few countries have shown greater sincerity of purpose and a higher quality of quiet determination than yours. Blessed with the wealth of natural resources, you have shown the world how a nation, by dint of hard work, by its unity, its sturdy moral qualities, its progres-sive yet modest outlook, its wide international sympathies and its neighbourliness, can raise itself to great heights, bringing happiness to many and fear to none among those who love peace and honour the freedom of others as they do their own. I am sure that we can look forward to a long period of friendship between our two coun-tries, and that in any joint moral undertaking to promote the welfare of mankind and good will and peace among nations, Pakistan and Canada will be more than friends. God bless your country and its people.

The Speakers of both the Canadian Houses of Parliament ac-knowledged the address of the Prime Minister of Pakistan with cordial remarks assuring him of the admiration and friendship Canadians hold for his country. The talk of the Honorable Elie Beauregard, Speaker of the Senate, follows.

Your Excellency, the Upper Chamber and the French-speaking people, on whose behalf I am now speaking, are pleased to welcome both yourself and your charming wife and collaborator, and to thank you for the friendly visit you have paid the Canadian Parliament as well as for the substantial speech you have delivered. In you we greet a distinguished representative of a Commonwealth nation which, in addition, is one of the world's greatest countries.

By its spiritual unity, based on the teachings and tradition of Islam, the sovereign state of Pakistan binds two territories that, oddly enough, are divided geographically. This thousand-year-old bond, of which religion and culture are the warp and woof, you recognize as stronger, as more imperious than that of nearness, of a single land.

Pakistan's evolution provides one of the most interesting chapters of world history. In a sort of prophetic vision, your great poet Iqbal foresaw the development which you have made it your mission to achieve.

Under your leadership, your country, which throughout the ages has known and absorbed many civilizations, has progressed rapidly in the economic field. Though this is somewhat contrary to our conception of a legendary and static Orient, we can but rejoice at its march towards progress and a better standard of living, benefits which are common to all true democracies.

Following in the footsteps of the illustrious Mohammed Ali Jinnah, you recognize, as the leader of your country, that your authority comes to you from the people. You have desired to establish your country's constitution on a democratic basis and to complete its independence by making its policy as one with its ideals.

Through your character and your culture, as well as through the exigencies of our time, you are enabled to understand to the full what democracy really means. You know that a strong nation is one in which the several units are made responsible for national development, by being called upon to participate in the administration of public affairs.

Your industrial and social program is commensurate to your overflowing personality. You are extending in the economic sphere the reform accomplished in the political field. Without breaking your age-long traditions, you are leading your people to the development of natural resources, big industry and world trade. Pakistan shall thus be a democratic, industrial and prosperous country.

May we, Excellency, greet in you the great architect of this national revival and offer you a tribute of admiration and the expression of our best wishes.

The talk of the Honorable W. Ross Macdonald, Speaker of the Canadian House of Commons, 31 May.

From time to time our parliament has been honoured by visits from internationally known statesmen. Once again this honour has come to us. Today we have had the privilege of receiving the Prime Minister of a new nation which has been formed by people of ancient lineage and great traditions. The history of our country is very short compared to that of the country of our distinguished visitor, but we are a few years older in the status of nationhood. We are both young nations. I am sure we were all very much pleased to hear our Prime Minister say that we are sister nations; and then, shortly after, we were happy indeed to hear our distinguished visitor say that we belong to the same family circle.

Pakistan and Canada have many things in common. Allow me to mention but one. Both countries are bordered by powerful nations which speak the same or a similar language and which have the same customs and traditions. Canada has lived in peace with her powerful neighbour for nearly 150 years. I am sure that I speak for all our members when I say that we hope our younger sister, Pakistan, will enjoy with her neighbour the same peaceful relations as her elder sister, Canada, has enjoyed with her neighbour.

Mr. Liaquat Ali Khan, may I express to you our admiration for the statesmanship which has already been demonstrated by you in facing the problems which have confronted you. We are deeply impressed by the high morale of your people and their faith in the belief that their new status as a sovereign independent nation will gradually bring to them a better way of life.

Mr. Liaquat Ali Khan, on behalf of the members of the Canadian House of Commons, I extend to you our deep appreciation for your very informative and inspiring address this afternoon. Our Prime Minister has asked you to convey a message to all your people. May I, as Speaker of the House of Commons, ask you upon your return to Pakistan to carry our greetings to your constituent assembly, and to tell your members how happy Canadians were today to have in their houses of parliament the Prime Minister of Pakistan.

The next day, 1 June 1950, Liaquat Ali Khan addressed the Canadian Club of Ottawa. Here again he is not introducing a relatively unknown country to strangers but rather, like one member of a family to another distant one, he explains the facts and conditions needed for current understanding.

WHAT CANADIANS SHOULD KNOW ABOUT PAKISTAN

I am conscious of the fact that in addressing this distinguished gathering I am talking to friends and to people who take a deep interest in international affairs. I would not, therefore, attempt on this occasion to adopt the tiresome course of introducing to you my country and its people or to tell you of the origin of our new State. But as I am assured of your friendship for Pakistan and your sympathetic understanding of our problems and aspirations, I would like to share some of these with you as friends generally do.

May I begin by reminding you that Pakistan is a Dominion within the Commonwealth of Nations. I say this to underline the fact that the Constitution under which we are at present operating is the Constitution bequeathed to us by the British, in the shape of the so-called Government of India Act passed by the British Parliament in 1935, although of course we have made certain changes in it to adapt it to our new status as a Dominion. This Constitution is federal in structure with five provinces which are autonomous in all matters except defence, foreign policy, communications and customs. Our new Constitution is on the anvil and our Constituent Assembly which consists of the elected representatives of the people is working on it. In the meantime, we continue to adjust the 1935 Constitution to meet the increasingly progressive requirements of a liberalized democracy. For example, in the new elections which are shortly to be held in one of our major provinces, it has been decided to have an adult franchise for men and women, which would be a considerable advance on the provisions of the 1935 act. The new Constitution is being shaped to conform more closely to the genius of our people than it was possible for a foreign government to have achieved. Enough work has already been done on it to show very clearly that it is democratic in all its basic conceptions, and regards fundamental human rights as amongst its cardinal principles. It ensures to the Muslims, who form the majority of our eighty million people, the right to order their lives in accordance with their faith but it also pledges to the minorities full and equal rights of citizenship and the complete freedom to profess and practise their religions. Furthermore, since Islam abhors the caste system, our new Constitution, and indeed our traditions and our practice, guarantee that, politically and socially, no human being in our State shall be regarded as being inferior or superior to others because of his birth or his profession. We call this the Muslim way of life because whatever the source from which other nations may have acquired the same beliefs, to the Muslims they have been propounded by their religion, of which they are an essential part. I consider these few words of explanation necessary in order to remove the misconception, if such a misconception exists anywhere, that Pakistan is, or plans to become, the stronghold of intolerance or medievalism. Our religion, as you know, does not recognise priesthood as necessary. It is hardly likely therefore that this would be laid down as the necessary qualification for a Cabinet Minister.

A word about our economic problems. In the economic field we had a very bad start. Under the British rule the Muslims were the poorer and the more backward of the two nations in the subcontinent. Trade and commerce were almost entirely in the hands of the Hindus and all the major industries were located in that part of the subcontinent which now forms the neighbouring dominion of India. When the subcontinent was partitioned the Hindu trading community and the Hindu technicians who were living in Pakistan abandoned our territory and migrated to India. Some Muslim traders, driven out of their ancestral homes in India, similarly migrated to Pakistan but they were fewer in number and were mostly

127

small businessmen with meagre experience. Along with them also came seven million refugees—mostly destitute farmers with no land or tools or cattle. These unexpected shocks to our economy, both because of the great gaps that appeared in our economic structure and the heavy strain that was placed on our resources and our two-month-old administrative machinery, were our greatest trial. What saved us was neither our administrative experience nor our skill—for we possessed little of either—but the determination, the unity and the self-sacrifice of our people. Our import and export trade revived quickly and strengthened our internal economy and foreign exchange position. Within a short time we established the State Bank of Pakistan to manage the currency of the country and to build up our banking structure, an Industrial Finance Corporation to help small and medium industries, a National Bank of Pakistan to fill up the gaps in our banking and undertake trading work in the districts on behalf of Government and a Refugee Finance Corporation to rehabilitate refugees in business and cottage industries.

We are an agricultural country with low productivity. We are therefore going ahead with irrigation projects to bring more land under the plough, with the purchase of tractors and modern implements, with the manufacture and import of fertilizers and with plans for cooperative farming. More than half the money allotted to development schemes is earmarked for projects which will help the expansion and modernization of agriculture. Cheap electrical power is the basic need of our country and the work in progress in this field is aimed at giving us by 1957 sufficient energy for our industrial requirements, for modernizing our agriculture and for setting up a country-wide network of cottage and small-scale industries. We are transforming our railways in order to be independent of coal as far as possible and we have considerably expanded our existing ports. . . .

Industrially we have a long way to go yet and have therefore made many provisions to create the necessary climate for investment of indigenous and foreign capital in industrial concerns. Needless to say, except for those very few industries which were state-controlled even under the British rule, all our industries are open to private enterprise.

By giving you this account of our efforts to raise the standard of living of our people, I wish to convey to you our great need and therefore our earnest desire for peace. I know that some friends have commented upon the heavy expenditure that we have incurred on defence. Their views, I am sure, would have been quite different had they known that when the Indo-Pakistan subcontinent was partitioned, we were allotted a certain share of the joint military equipment and stores, but that the greater bulk of this share has been refused to us. We had, therefore, to equip our army by fresh purchases from other sources. We have no aggressive designs and certainly no territorial ambitions. We do not aim to be among the athletes of the world. We only wish to keep healthy and fit.

As a friend and as a member of the Commonwealth I know that Canada is interested in Indo-Pakistan relations. These have not been free from anxiety. . . . Recently the two governments have entered into an agreement, regarding the treatment of the minorities in their respective territories, which has been welcomed by millions of people in both India and Pakistan. This agreement, I am glad to say, is working satisfactorily and has improved the general atmosphere appreciably. There are some major matters, however, still in dispute between our two countries. Foremost amongst them is the problem of Kashmir. There is luckily an international agreement between Pakistan and India that the question of Kashmir's accession to India or Pakistan shall be decided by a free and impartial plebiscite of the people of Kashmir themselves. By this we stand; but we have never wished to conceal our anxiety over the long delay that has taken place in holding such a plebiscite. At the time of the British withdrawal, there were six hundred odd princely states in the subcontinent. Had the same principle been applied to Kashmir as has been applied to the other princely states, Kashmir would have joined Pakistan and there would have been no problem today. For geographically, economically, culturally and strategically, Kashmir, eighty per cent of whose population is Muslim, is an integral part of Pakistan. Nevertheless, we have agreed to accept the democratic decision of the people of Kashmir whatever it may be. On this we are all agreed and on this there cannot possibly be any compromise. On the intermediate points of difference each causing further delay and more heart-burning, Pakistan has always been willing to accept mediation, or arbitration. Indeed Pakistan has been willing to accept these as a method of settling all disputes. What else can Pakistan do to assure the world of its peaceful intentions and its desire for the welfare of both countries? But to force or coercion we can never submit.

We strongly believe in peace and stability in Asia and are determined to throw all our weight to help maintain stability in our continent, so far as it lies in our power to do so. Our resolve stems from two considerations. Firstly, peace in Asia is essential for our own progress. We did not struggle to achieve freedom merely to enjoy the sight of our flag or the sound of our national anthem. We longed for freedom because our people were suppressed and poor and our physical, mental and moral resources lay untapped. We could be in no hurry to throw away the chance of developing them, now that we have the chance. Therefore we are resolved to defend both peace and our freedom. Secondly, peace and stability in Asia are, we believe, essential for world-peace although from this point of view the under-developed countries of Asia cannot, without international cooperation and without sharing the experience and the technical skill of the more advanced countries of the world, develop themselves sufficiently quickly to resolve the menacing economic equilibrium that exists in the world, and thus to establish mental and moral security. Any kind of disruption in Asia we regard with apprehension. We can neither start a world war as such or stop it by ourselves. We do, however, regard it as our moral responsibility to keep our own house in order, to defend our own freedom against aggression from any quarter, and sincerely and earnestly to go ahead with the task of developing our resources in cooperation with the peace-loving nations of the world. We are proud—pardonably proud I hope—of the fact that democracy, in the political, social and economic fields, is with us not a new creed but a matter of religious conviction, that there is no free democracy in Asia whose people are more unified and that we believe in God and His supreme sovereignty and regard our faith to be our greatest safeguard against ideological confusion and our greatest strength in combating any difficulties that the future may discover to us. We know that the people of Canada also hold these aims to be dear to them and have faith in us. We bless your efforts as I hope you will bless ours.

On 2 June in Kingston, Ontario, Liaquat Ali Khan delivered the
last of the formal addresses made on his trip to America. He
spoke to the delegates of the National Conference of Canadian
Universities, and very naturally the nature of his speech reflects
to some extent the nature of his audience. Therefore, although
the title of his address is similar to the titles of others and a large
part of his time is given to subject matter previously discussed
(and therefore omitted here), the concluding emphasis is placed
on his concept of education for Pakistan and the part education
can play in the peace of the world and the future of his country.

PAKISTAN'S ROLE IN THE MODERN WORLD

I consider myself extremely fortunate that my visit to Canada, which I owe to the kind hospitality of the Canadian Government, should have taken place at a time which has made it possible for me to address a distinguished assembly such as yours.

As you probably know I have recently concluded a somewhat quick but fairly extensive tour of the United States of America. To visit Canada as well as the United States of America in one, almost continuous journey has enabled me, in quick succession, to see two great countries who have won for themselves a position of great pre-eminence in world affairs.

My visit to Canada, though tantalizingly brief, has I am glad to say, contributed very substantially towards my understanding of the bearings of my country in the world situation. During the course of my travels both in the United States and in Canada I have had valuable opportunities of discussing many questions of mutual concern with eminent men, educators, civic leaders and students of international affairs. Although I sometimes felt that people in this hemisphere regarded the heart of the Asiatic continent where my country is situated to be more distant and remote than we at that end regard your part of the world to be, I have been heartened nevertheless to find a keen interest in the growth of the new democracies in Asia.

This has been amply demonstrated to me, among other things, by the recurring question: "What is the role that Pakistan hopes to play in the modern world?" The words have varied but the essence of the question has been more or less the same. I presume that this question will be of interest to you also, for I know that as educators who have a great part to play in shaping the future of the world by guiding and moulding the minds of men and women, it is of paramount importance to you to study the political and social forces that are at work in the world determining the ebb and flow of civilisation and thus the very context in which your noble task has to be done. Above all I know that you, for reasons higher and more fundamental than is given to most men to perceive, are interested in world peace. I will therefore try to interpret the facts of the situation in which our country is placed and will try to show their bearing on the questions which come to the forefront whenever two freedom-loving, peace-loving countries such as yours and mine share their confidences with each other. . . .

What place, you might ask, does education occupy in the scheme of our aspirations? I will answer this question very briefly. Education occupies the highest place but only if by education we understand equipping the people technically, mentally and morally to be useful to themselves and to the society in which they find themselves,—and not merely a process which, as in the past, may be unrelated to their national needs and ideals. First and foremost therefore education must have a moral aim or else it will be out of tune with the genius of our people. Besides this it must on the one hand offer the fullest scope for the development of our culture and on the other take into account our extreme backwardness in the technological field. In other words it must aim at a new synthesis which should equip us for the modern world without destroying the attractive features of our ancient civilisation. Lastly, it must be aimed at removing the appallingly high percentage of illiteracy

133

amongst the masses. It is here where the difficulties are the greatest and constitute the highest challenge to our endeavour. For in countries like ours where mass ignorance and mass poverty exist side by side, the real obstacle would be not so much the lack of schools or the lack of teachers, as the paucity of pupils. As long as the parents are poor, a child is more valuable to them at home than in the school and education has little attraction for them unless it is directly and immediately related to their economic betterment.

The basis of discontent in Asia is economic. So is the basis of all cures, real or spurious, which are offered for its removal. It is by their efforts in the economic field that Governments in Asia which have democratic ideals or in other words aspire to be governments for the people, should judge themselves and will eventually be judged by the world. It is a matter of some satisfaction to us therefore that Pakistan has a sound economy and the Government is therefore in a position to go ahead with its policies for economic and industrial development with the full confidence and co-operation of the people.

But in the task of the economic rehabilitation of the people, Pakistan, like most Asiatic countries, can only go a certain distance and no further—that is to say, no further without international co-operation. The question that we should all ask ourselves is: can Pakistan make up for the lost centuries of technological advance and industrial development sufficiently quickly to give weight and substance to its contribution to world peace? The clear answer is that without international co-operation few countries by themselves can today discharge their responsibility as effectively and as quickly as they may desire. So far as the prospects of an immediate world war are concerned it will be nothing new or profound if I were to say that it is not the people in Asia who can pronounce upon it with authority. Our responsibility is to keep our own house in order, to go ahead with the enormous task in front of us, of developing our resources, of educating our people and of demonstrating to them in actual practice the benefits of democracy. Whoever helps us in promoting these aims will help us to help peace.

If I have been able to convey to you the strong urge for self-government, self-development, freedom, democracy and liberty among the people of Pakistan which achieved the unique phenomenon of creating on the map of Asia a new State of eighty million people, it will not be difficult for you to infer that we passionately desire peace in order to accomplish that for which we founded our country. You desire peace too—in order to continue to enjoy the fruits of the great civilisation which you have built up with your love of liberty and your rigorous moral qualities. We desire it to have the barest chance to translate some of our dreams into reality. We sincerely hope and believe that with your wisdom, experience and technical knowledge you will not hesitate to step out into the vast constructive fields that are open to you in all parts of the world and where alone the foundations of a lasting peace can be firmly and securely laid. In such a task you will find Pakistan not only a friend but an enthusiastic comrade.

*The brief address of Mr. George F. Kennan, at the Town Hall
Dinner, 8 May 1950, setting forth some of America's problems
and assuring the Prime Minister of America's goodwill, is here
printed as an*

EPILOGUE

I do not need to assure the Prime Minister and the Begum Liaquat
again how delighted we all are that they could accept the President's
invitation to visit the United States and how welcome they are in
this country.

For those of us who are professionally concerned in foreign affairs,
there is a particular interest and satisfaction in the opportunity to
meet personally with the Prime Minister of Pakistan. Why is this?
It is because in the contacts and dealings between our own Government and the Government of Pakistan today we have the unique
opportunity of creating from the beginning a new international relationship—a relationship between great peoples whose feelings
toward each other are not burdened by any unhappy relics of the
past, by any bitter memories or misunderstandings, by any rivalries
or jealousies or frictions. We have here an opportunity which does
not often come to nations: an opportunity to shape a new international relationship, to shape it in such a way as to avoid those things
which have troubled relations between nations in the past, to make it
a well-founded and solid structure, a structure designed for the
future.

It may seem at first glance as though, of the two of us, it were only
our friends in Pakistan who have the opportunity and the necessity
to create a foreign policy and a system of international relationships
from the ground up, and in the strict sense this is true. Yet the
changes which we in this country have experienced in our world
environment and in the demands which it places upon us within

recent years are such that it is not too much to say that we too have in many respects had to begin at the bottom as though we were a new country and to create these things for ourselves out of our own best judgment and against a very shallow and brief background of experience. The changes brought about in world society by the two world wars and the period between them left us suddenly in a position, after the termination of hostilities five years ago, so different from that to which we were accustomed that it was in a sense like being born anew into a new world of reality.

One of the hardest of our problems, and one which I think is without precedent in world history, has been the tremendous disparity, partly temporary and partly also of a long-term nature, between our own great economic strength and the difficulties which many other peoples were experiencing in the economic field. There was a great problem as to what the proper relationship should be between a country such as our own and other free countries who were in an entirely different position. This involved for us heavy problems of wisdom and discretion in the application of our own strength and in our willingness to participate in the solution of world problems. We are only now beginning to become generally aware of the delicacy of this relationship between ourselves and other peoples and of the dangers which it harbors. We are coming to learn that there is no special form of assistance which is not also a form of responsibility; that every special relationship we create with another country is not just a fact in itself but also a precedent for the future in the minds of our own people as well as in the minds of people elsewhere; that whenever we offer a reason as to why something should be done in the case of one country we must also have reasons why it should not be done in the case of fifty others. We know now that we must think not only about the psychological repercussions of the beginning of any program of special collaboration but also about the repercussions of its termination.

In short, we are becoming wiser and more balanced in our thinking about these matters, and are beginning to realize that if we are to play our part in the world effectively, we must do so with great prudence and restraint and observe the utmost care not to enter into relationships which might become the subjects of misunderstandings either here or in the partner-country or elsewhere, or which we could not be sure of carrying through to a conclusion satisfactory to all concerned. This has no particular application to our relations with Pakistan. I mention it because it is so important a part of our attempt to find a correct and constructive relation with our world environment in general, and because we want our friends to understand the complexities of our situation and to refrain from expecting us to do things which we cannot do, not just in our bilateral relations with them, but in the general exercise of our responsibilities as a world power.

You will note I say our friends must not expect us to do things which we cannot do. It is no less important that they should not expect us to be things which we cannot be. You, Mr. Prime Minister, are soon to have an opportunity to get a closer glimpse of this country of ours about which so much is spoken that is favorable, but perhaps more that is unfavorable, in the lands beyond our borders. We are happy that you are to have this opportunity. We know that many sides of our life still have an unfinished aspect, that they are in a process of change and development, and are not universally pleasing or readily comprehensible. There is much about our society which many of us feel could be and should be improved. But we are convinced that whoever looks deeply and without prejudice at our people and their institutions will understand that here, as elsewhere, there is a reason for everything, and a reason entitled to respect. It is this respect for the origins of our civilization and for the magnitude of our American experiment which we seek from others: not sentimental enthusiasm or imitation.

In general, we do not believe that a sound and fruitful international relationship demands a great intimacy or identity of taste in such matters as the customs and habits of domestic life. We can conceive that others might not want to live as we live, and vice versa.

139

We think that what is required is only that one nation should respect the privacy of another nation in these matters—and by privacy I mean its right to pursue its customs and its beliefs without criticism or interference from outside, as long as these things do not impinge themselves in unfortunate ways on the international community.

We are prepared to judge our friends by their conduct in their relations with us and to be judged in that way ourselves. With these things in mind, we see no reason why we should not be able to develop with the people of Pakistan, for whom there are no feelings in this country other than ones of deep friendship and the most fervent good wishes for a successful and glorious national future, a relationship so happy and so fruitful that it will constitute an example in this international community which is searching so desperately for stability and peace.

The Prime Minister may be assured that in the effort to establish this relationship he will have our loyal and competent support.

We know that his visit is designed to contribute, and has already contributed, to this end, and we are grateful to him for taking the trouble to make it.

APPENDIX

An Address by Begum Liaquat Ali Khan

*During the visit of Prime Minister Liaquat Ali Khan and the
Begum to the United States and Canada, the Begum was almost
as busy a public speaker as her husband. She spoke informally
at numerous gatherings across the United States and in Canada,
and she delivered several formal addresses of weight and importance. Notable among the latter were her speeches at Hood College, Frederick, Maryland, on 5 May; before the American
Women's Association at Washington on 6 May; at Town Hall,
New York, on 10 May; again, on 10 May, at Barnard College of
Columbia University; at Wellesley College on 25 May; and on
the radio in Canada on 31 May. In all these addresses she at-
tempted to explain what the women of her country had done
and were doing in these critical years of their country's existence
and to make clear the new horizons opened for Muslim women
by national independence. Printed here is the Town Hall speech
of 10 May 1950, the longest and perhaps the most comprehensive
of all her addresses. It has been abridged slightly to avoid repetition of details covered in her husband's speeches.*

WHAT THE WOMEN OF PAKISTAN ARE DOING

In coming to the Town Hall today I do not feel a stranger. On the
other hand, I feel that I already know you as I had the pleasure of
meeting some of your members in Karachi during the last winter.
We had, in my house, a very free and frank panel discussion which
I and my colleagues found very illuminating. In that discussion a
large number of women workers of Pakistan took part and they all
have a vivid recollection of the earnestness and frankness shown by
those of your members who came to Karachi. Seeing those familiar
faces around me I feel among friends.

I am going to talk to you about the women of Pakistan and what
they are doing. Before I do that, however, I should like to point out
why Pakistan is likely to be of interest to the people of America.

It is a truism to say that during the last one hundred years, and
particularly during the last forty years or so, the world has become

142

a very small place. The old concept of distance has disappeared never to come back. Whatever happens in one corner of the globe has its repercussions with surprising rapidity in all countries of the world. For the first time the world has, for good or evil, become one. We are all now in the same boat to swim or sink together.

A great majority of human beings of the world believe in the democratic way of life. America, which is the greatest democracy in the world, is in the vanguard of those nations who want to preserve democracy. The eighty million people of Pakistan are determined to follow a democratic way of life, and to work for peace and the preservation of democracy. America is one of the most advanced countries in the world; Pakistan is striving to become one. They both have the same ideals.

The organisation which I have the privilege to address today is working for the same ends. The very idea of a Town Hall is a democratic one. In dictatorships or autocracies there are no discussions and no arguments. There are those who give orders and those who have to carry them out. There is no real freedom for the individual and no free play for the human intellect. That is why all dictatorships have the germs of decay in them and are bound, in the long run, to break up.

Those of us who believe that, of all the systems of Government, the democratic is the most preferable, must not forget, however, that it is not a perfect system, and secondly that a living democracy should provide a continually expanding horizon of freedom to its members.

We must remember that a democratic system is not as secure as some of us are apt to believe. The last war made it clear that it is the easiest thing for a democracy to slip into a dictatorship. A people has not only to fight for freedom but to continue to fight for the preservation of liberty. The price of liberty, as we have been reminded so often, is eternal vigilance.

The people of Pakistan have learnt this during the last two and a half years. They won their freedom after making tremendous sacrifices, and they have begun to appreciate the fact that in order to preserve the integrity of their country and a free society in Pakistan they will have to work continuously and work very hard. There never comes a time in the life of an individual or the life of a nation when it can sit back and say "I have done enough; I can rest." Ceasing to work and ceasing to struggle is a negation of life itself, or perhaps I had better say, a negation of all progress, because it is one of the laws of Nature that you either go forward or you go back; it is never given to you to stand still. When you have the illusion of standing still you are actually going backward. . . .

I shall discuss the educational problems of Pakistan, particularly those relating to the women of my country. Three hundred years ago Pakistan had a completely medieval society which has been gradually breaking up under the impact of English rule and today it is a curious hodgepodge of the modern and the medieval. The women of Pakistan have been left behind in whatever progress the country has made towards modernity. Theirs is the responsibility to run a house efficiently and economically and to bring up the children. In their homes they are supreme but outside their homes they are completely helpless because they have had little or no occasion to leave the home. A tradition was established under which it was considered derogatory for a woman to earn her living as it was thought that the proper place for her was her own home. Not only did this erroneous conception of women's duties and responsibilities result in the assignment of a somewhat inferior role to a woman compared to a man, but it also led to an embargo being placed on her participating fully in the national life. With the creation of Pakistan it was felt all round that it was wasteful to have half the population of the country doing relatively unimportant work. There has been a welcome change in this outlook and although established conventions and traditions die hard an ever increasing number of young women are coming forward to contribute their might to the refashioning of the social structure of the country.

It would not be inappropriate to say a word about how the change took place. On the eve of partition in the Eastern part of the Punjab which fell to the share of India a very large-scale massacre of Muslims took place. This resulted in the death of nearly one million Muslims, men, women and children, and the flight of seven million more from their homes towards Pakistan. Between August 1947 and January 1948 these uprooted people poured into Pakistan. They had lost their all. There was hardly a family which had not lost at least one of its members and in many cases he happened to be the head of the family. There were hundreds of thousands of children who had lost their parents, women who had lost their husbands and other relatives and old couples who had lost all their grown-up children. This overwhelming mass of humanity had to be fed, clothed and otherwise looked after. All the schools, colleges and other available buildings had become camps or hospitals. Even then there was not enough room for the refugees. They were lying on the roadsides, and in the open fields, in the scorching heat of the sun during the burning days of August, and in the cold winter nights of December. Government had not yet had time to organise its own machinery. Most of the senior administrative officers who had been non-Muslims had left at the time of partition. The communications system had been brought to a standstill by these large-scale migrations. Unless all the Pakistani, men and women, came forward to help there was no way of solving the problem.

I was in Lahore, the capital of the Western and Pakistan section of the Punjab, when the refugees were coming in from India. It then occurred to me that a national emergency like this was probably the best occasion for bringing the women of Pakistan into the field of active welfare work. This would not only be of considerable value to the country but would also give them confidence and experience of welfare work.

Accordingly I organised the Pakistan Women's Volunteer Service and appealed for workers. The response was extremely heartening. Hundreds of women of all ages and from all classes came forward to do whatever they could. They were organised into batches and assigned to camps and hospitals. There was no work which they

145

did not do or which they considered demeaning. I must confess that the devotion to duty and disregard of personal comfort which was shown by the women of Pakistan came as a very pleasant surprise to everybody and earned the gratitude not only of the refugees but of the Government as well. When epidemics of cholera and smallpox were raging in the camps the welfare workers went on with their work, completely disregarding their own safety. Throughout this period, girls went from house to house collecting food and clothing for the refugees. Though they were often put to a great deal of trouble they were always cheerful. They never complained.

When the members of the P.W.V.S. had been working for about five or six months they felt that they could do more useful work if they were given some kind of organised basic training. In order to fulfil this need I organised the Pakistan Women's National Guard in January, 1948. The basic course consisted of physical training, nursing and elementary welfare work. Hundreds of workers completed this course and many of them took up the advanced course which included advanced nursing, ambulance driving, typing, shorthand, signalling and A.R.P. At the moment we have about twenty-four hundred women as members of the P.W.N.G. They are organised in three battalions by geographic distribution. The number of women who have completed their courses and left the organisation for "inactive duty" is considerable.

When the work of the settlement of refugees had eased somewhat, it was felt that a separate organisation was needed to take up the work of a more permanent nature. To fulfil this need, the All Pakistan Women's Association was created. All the smaller organisations doing welfare work for women are affiliated to A.P.W.A.

This Association has organised adult and literacy centers, primary schools, industrial homes for widows and Pakistan Cottage Industries.

The industrial homes have proved very useful as they have not only provided work for a large number of women, who had no other means of livelihood, but in addition they have served as training centres for those women who wanted to learn new professions like tailoring, dress making, needlepoint, etc. Pakistan Cottage Industries has been organised with a view to helping our national cottage industries which were slowly dying out. The livelihood of a very large number of people in Pakistan depends on cottage industries. The establishment of these centres in various provinces has already given much encouragement to workers in the villages. Our intention is not only to provide facilities for the marketing of these goods but to give the workers new designs and new methods.

The women of Pakistan are now very eager to play their full part in the building up of their nation. There are now a much larger number of Muslim girls who are being trained as doctors, nurses, teachers, etc.

Of course, the number of these is nowhere near that which is required for a population of eighty million, but the beginning is heartening and very promising.

As you will have gathered the problems that face our country are so numerous, vital and complex that here I can but touch upon some of them that are of particular interest to us as women and on which we are at present working.

Far and away the most important problem, and one of the biggest and toughest that we are tackling, is that of national health. I do not for one moment pretend that conditions in this are even adequate, much less ideal—but that is both our problem and our challenge, which we, the women of Pakistan, are trying to meet in some measure through our various social service organisations and groups such as the A.P.W.A., and by individual and personal effort and example wherever and whenever possible. Our aim is to make our people "health-conscious" and then they themselves will see to it that they get what they need and want. Ignorance, poverty, distress, and indifference have to be fought and overcome in addition to the difficulties of lack of funds, personnel, equipment and other disabilities. Our hospitals are too few in number and suffer from all

147

these disabilities, and it has been an almost herculean task to bring them up to their present standards of work and efficiency.

You must bear in mind three things as we present and discuss these problems: first, that we are but two and a half years old politically; second, that we inherited an almost completely unfurnished house, so to speak, for what little furniture was in it was extremely poor, meagre and utterly inadequate to meet the normal needs envisaged by the conditions of the Partition; third, that the Kashmir problem has absorbed and is still absorbing an enormous proportion of our time, energy and money, all of which might otherwise be used for constructive national work.

I mention these facts, not in a spirit of bitterness or recrimination, but with the intention of clarifying our position, for it is only then that we can evaluate the work we have clearly done, and the magnitude of the work which still remains for us to do. As a single example, let me tell you of the Jinnah Central Hospital in Karachi, of whose Managing Committee I am a member. This was a small British R.A.F. Hospital put up during the last war and evacuated at Partition. When we took it over, at the height of the refugee influx, the medicines it possessed could have been contained in one small wall-cupboard, the nursing staff was down to about six or eight members, and the bed and house linen was being supplemented by what one voluntary lady worker was begging from house to house or bringing in herself. In Eastern Pakistan there are only two thousand hospital beds for a population of forty-five million. I was forced to arrange to have untrained women volunteers help daily in the hospitals, giving what assistance they could and learning the elements of the work as fast and as best they could in the midst of the terrific rush of work. Women also visited refugee camps and other places with medical supplies, food and clothing. The lack of trained nurses was a severe handicap, for nursing was not a profession taken up by Muslim girls. Realising the vital importance of such a training both for our girls and for the country, I appealed for Muslim girls of good family and education to come forward for training. This was no easy matter, for it entailed a clash with old prejudices and customs; it required my personal appeal not only to the girls, but to their families who had to be convinced and assured that the general living, work and social conditions attached to nursing would be overhauled and bettered. Finally, we were able to get a fairly good response, and have been able to arrange to have well qualified foreign nurses come over to train the girls in the Pakistan hospitals, and to send Pakistani nurses abroad for training. The nursing situation is still very far from adequate or satisfactory, but in spite of tremendous difficulties a beginning has been made and that, to my mind, is very important.

The same difficulties and inadequacies prevail with regard to our schools. All the larger, older, better-equipped, better-known schools, colleges, training centres, libraries, museums, etc., fell to India's share, and even the shares of books, equipment, instruments, art treasures, etc., which should have come to us, according to the terms of the Partition, we have not received. Such schools and colleges as did exist already in the Pakistan area were quite inadequate to cope with the enormously increased demand placed upon them, and in a number of cases were compelled to put up temporary tent structures and work in two to three shifts a day. My eldest son attends what is considered one of the older and better schools of Karachi, and there, the Principal informed me, they were having to cope with over eight hundred boys and girls in a school originally built for and catering to some two to three hundred children. It is the same in every school and college. Obviously this is no ideal situation, but I am definitely of the opinion that bad as it is, it is preferable to keeping the children without any education until such time as we can provide them with palatial buildings, expert staff, modern equipment and all the things we do wish them to have and know they should have. This may not be possible for a considerable period of time, but our youth cannot wait idly by. They must carry on with whatever limited resources we have at our disposal for the time being. In the meantime, we are trying to open more schools wherever possible, and plans are under way for a really up to date, first rate public school. We feel strongly also that our system of education should be orientated to conform both to the needs of a modern, practical and progressive world and to the ideals of a truly Islamic State in such a world.

In Pakistan we attach a great deal of importance to religion and we want to build up our country as an Islamic State. I must explain that we are not going in for any kind of domination by priests or fanaticism or intolerance. These have nothing whatever to do with Islam. What we wish to emphasise are the basic Islamic principles of equality, brotherhood and social and economic justice. We believe that a civilisation or a society which concerns itself with material things alone cannot endure. Human needs are not entirely material, but are also spiritual and they must both be satisfied if an individual or a society is to be a balanced one.

In other words, a human being must know that his whole existence is geared to something higher; something which is higher and yet has a very intimate connection with his day-to-day existence. We Muslims believe that the universe belongs to God and that human beings can find real happiness and the deepest kind of contentment only if they submit to the will of God. Islam does not believe in the renunciation of this world. It insists that only a good citizen, a good neighbour, a good husband or a good mother can be a good Muslim. The highest kind of saintliness is that which is practised by a citizen who is honest, kind and charitable in his dealings with his fellow beings. . . .

These are the principles on which alone a free, stable and progressive society can be built; and these are the principles on which we want to base our education. Education, if it is to achieve its purpose, must make an individual conscious of his relationship with other human beings and his responsibilities towards his community. Everybody must feel responsible for everybody else.

One of the great tragedies of the modern world is the fact that many human beings feel that they are not responsible for others but only for themselves. This attitude is responsible for a great deal of neurosis in the world today which results in endless strife. Human beings must learn once again that cooperation rather than competition is the real key to the solution of many problems which face the world today. We must educate the future generations into a spirit of cooperative enterprise.

For Pakistan which is starting almost from scratch this might seem too ambitious a programme. We are nothing if not ambitious. We are confident that with the help of God we shall achieve our ideals.

Pakistan, being a young country, is willing, I should say even anxious, to learn from every country. America, being the greatest democracy in the world, has a great deal to teach us. American democracy has weathered many storms and stood the test of time. It has conducted a very interesting experiment in democratic education on a gigantic scale. I am sure we will benefit a great deal by making a close study of American conditions. . . .